Charging into Immortality: The Life and Legacy of George Pickett

By Charles River Editors

About Charles River Editors

Charles River Editors was founded by Harvard and MIT alumni to provide superior editing and original writing services, with the expertise to create digital content for publishers across a vast range of subject matter. In addition to providing original digital content for third party publishers, Charles River Editors republishes civilization's greatest literary works, bringing them to a new generation via ebooks.

Visit charlesrivereditors.com for more information.

Introduction

George Pickett (1825-1875)

Before July 3, 1863, George Pickett was best known among his comrades for finishing last in his class at West Point, being a jocular but courageous soldier, and his carefully perfumed locks. As part of West Point's most famous Class of 1846, Pickett was classmates with men like Stonewall Jackson and George McClellan, and despite his poor class standing he distinguished himself fresh out of school during the Mexican-American War.

Pickett's reputation for bravery extended into the early years of the Civil War, to the extent that former West Point classmate George McClellan wrote, "Perhaps there is no doubt that he was the best infantry soldier developed on either side during the Civil War." A native Virginian, the impeccably styled Pickett represented all of the antebellum South's most cherished traits, and as such he was a "beau-ideal" Confederate soldier.

After proving himself a capable brigadier during the Peninsula Campaign, during which he was wounded and forced to recuperate, Pickett was given command of a division in Longstreet's corps of the Confederate Army of Northern Virginia, putting him in position for a rendez-vous with destiny. Today Pickett is best remembered for the charge that has taken his name and is now remembered as the most famous assault of the Civil War. Having failed to dislodge the Union

Army of the Potomac on either flank during the first two days at Gettysburg, Lee ordered a charge of nearly 15,000 at the center of the lines. The attack is now considered the high water mark of the Confederacy, spelling the South's doom with the failed charge and the loss at Gettysburg. Pickett's division was so decimated by the charge that when Lee asked him to reform his division in case of a Union counterattack, Pickett is alleged to have responded, "I have no division!"

Pickett would later become notorious for the loss at the Battle of Five Forks that helped the Union break the siege at Petersburg and force Lee's surrender a week later at Appomattox. Rumors that Pickett and Lee intensely disliked each other have persisted ever since, with Pickett reputed to have said after the war "that man destroyed my division." Ironically, Pickett's Charge was always a sore subject with the general even though it was intended to be a tribute to the soldiers of his division for advancing the furthest during the doomed assault, and Pickett offered one of the most candid quotes after the Civil War on the topic of who was to blame for the loss at Gettysburg: "I've always thought the Yankees had something to do with it."

Charging Into Immortality chronicles the life and career of Pickett and examines the controversy and legacy surrounding his Civil War record and the charge named after him. Along with accounts of Pickett's Charge and pictures of important people, places, and events in his life, you will learn about General Pickett like you never have before.

Section of the Gettysburg cyclorama depicting the High Water Mark of Pickett's Charge

Chapter 1: Early Years

The Pickett Family Tree

George Edward Pickett was born in January 1825 in Richmond, Virginia, the first of eight children born to Robert and Mary Johnston Pickett, one of the influential "first families" of Virginia that traced its arrival from England to 1635. George's siblings were listed as: Elizabeth Johnston (1826—1827), Mary Seldon (1829—1830), Olivia (1831—1832), Virginia (1833--? [survived to adulthood]), Mary (1835—1836), Robert Johnston (1837—1838), and Charles (1840--?). George, Mary, and Robert were the only Pickett children to survive to adulthood.

While numerous biographic sources cite George Pickett's date of birth as January 28, 1825, the Pickett Society provides the following: "According to the Rector's Register of Marriages, Burials and Christenings at St. John's Episcopal Church on Church Hill in Richmond, Virginia, George Edward Pickett was baptized on March 10, 1827 with his parents, Robert and Mary giving the birth date of their son as January 16, 1825."[1] Additionally, the Pickett Society has a letter from the Virginia Historical Society that confirms this information.

George's mother, Mary Johnston, was the daughter of Robert and Elizabeth McCaw Johnston, and his maternal grandmother, Robert Johnston, was the son of James and Mary Bryson Johnston of Byselaw, Scotland. Mary McCaw, George's grandmother, was the daughter of Dr. James and Elizabeth Brough McCaw of Heighten, Galloway, Scotland.

Pickett was born in Richmond at the home (and business location) of his maternal grandfather Robert Johnston on the north side of Main Street, between 10th and 11th Streets. As members of Old Virginia "aristocracy", George was known by if not related to virtually everybody of importance east of Richmond, Virginia.

George was also a cousin of future Confederate general Henry Heth, whose division started the Battle of Gettysburg on the morning of July 1, 1863 when it came into contact with John Buford's cavalry.

Education

Despite being a well regarded family in Richmond society, there are few records of George's early life, leaving historians to surmise that he was something like he was during his teen years at West Point. If so, he was no doubt a mischievous and popular child who loved to play pranks.

Information on George's education is also sparse. , As with most details of George's early life,

---

[1]   Pickett Society website.

there is virtually no specific information available regarding his early education. All that is known with relative certainty is that he was educated locally in the Richmond area before travelling to Springfield, Illinois to study law. That destination ensured that he crossed paths with local lawyer Abraham Lincoln, which gave rise to a popular but discredited rumor that it was Lincoln who secured Pickett's appointment to West Point.

Following attendance at one of the Lancastrian Schools (the "Lancastrian" System was structured so that more advanced students could teach less advanced students, thus enabling a small number of adult masters to educate large numbers of students at low cost), George attended Richmond Academy, and then West Point Military Academy, in New York.

Chapter 2: West Point

After studying law for an unknown period of time, 17 year old George Edward Pickett was appointed to West Point by Illinois Congressman John T. Stuart, a friend of Pickett's uncle and a law partner of future President Abraham Lincoln. Popular legend inspired in part by Pickett's widow had it that Lincoln secured the appointment, but as an Illinois State Legislator Lincoln could not have nominated candidates (though it has been suggested he may have offered George advice after he was accepted).

Pickett entered West Point in 1842, and he would go on to be remembered as one of a handful of West Point men who became important generals in the Civil War. The future generals' years at West Point became a source of colorful stories about the men who would become Civil War legends. In fact, Pickett would be a member of the Academy's most famous class. The Class of 1846 included a shy kid named Thomas Jonathan Jackson who made few friends and struggled with his studies, finishing 17th in his class 15 years before becoming Stonewall. Also in that class was A.P. Hill, who was already in love with the future wife of George McClellan, a young prodigy who finished second in the class of 1846. Other classes were full of colorful stories and important connections. A clerical error by West Point administrators ensured that Hiram Ulysses Grant forever became known as Ulysses S. Grant, and years after Robert E. Lee met Albert Sidney Johnston and Jefferson Davis at West Point, George H. Thomas and William Tecumseh Sherman met each other and Richard S. Ewell. Years after Pickett and the Class of 1846 left, it was followed by classes including Pickett's fellow division commander John Bell Hood, Union general Phil Sheridan and James Birdseye McPherson, who would become the only commanding general of a Union army to die in a Civil War battle when he fell in 1864 during Sherman's Atlanta Campaign.

Naturally, the popular and mischievous Pickett added to the lore of his famous class. The young McClellan developed a lifelong friendship with Pickett and later wrote of him in a letter to his wife, "[George] was, he is, and he will always be—even were his pistol pointed at my heart—my dear, loved friend."[2] But while McClellan was nearly a model student, Pickett was known for being more preoccupied with playing hooky at a local bar than his studies, and he became known as a "Dandy" prone to playing pranks. George was once described as "a man of ability, but belonging to a cadet set that appeared to have no ambition for class standing and wanted to do only enough study to secure their graduation."[3] Still, at a time in the Academy's history when one third of the class typically dropped out or failed due to excessive demerits, Pickett managed to do just enough in his studies to graduate, finishing dead last in his class. He would share the honor with another famous and flamboyant general who played a crucial role on the final day of the Battle of Gettysburg: George Armstrong Custer.

Referred to today by the dubious designation "goat" (chosen for the animal's stubbornness and tenacity) in West Point jargon, the term predicted its holder would be relegated to an obscure post with little opportunity to advance. But Pickett and his classmates lucked out by graduating shortly after war broke in Mexico. While men like Robert E. Lee bristled during peacetime service, the Mexican-American War allowed recent graduates a chance to fight right away, regardless of their class rank.

Chapter 3: Life Before the Civil War

The Mexican-American War

Ranking 59 out of 59 students in the Class of 1846, George was commissioned brevet Second Lieutenant in the U. S. Eighth Infantry Regiment.

Getting his first exposure to combat during the Mexican-American War, brevet Second Lieutenant George Edward Pickett participated in fighting from Vera Cruz (a 20 day siege lasting from March 9-29, 1847) to Mexico City, receiving praise and promotion for gallantry after the Battle of Churubusco (August of 1847).

In the Battle of Chapultepec, September 12-13, 1847, the Eighth Infantry Regiment made an assault up a hill, and at the front carrying the regiment's colors was Major James Longstreet. The color bearer who holds the flag marches front and center and is unarmed, making it the most dangerous position in 19th century warfare, and one that requires incredible bravery. During the charge, Longstreet was severely wounded in the thigh with a musket ball, and as he fell, he handed the flag off to Pickett. Pickett carried the American flag over the wall, was wounded, fought his way to the roof of the palace, tore down the enemy flag, and then replaced it with "Old Glory" to proclaim its surrender. Pickett received a brevet promotion to Captain, and both he and Longstreet earned reputations at Mexico that would allow them to command brigades

---

[2]   Gaffney, P. and D. Gaffney. *The Civil War: Exploring History One Week at a Time.* Page 84.

[3]   Gardner, *The Memoirs of Brigadier General William Passmore Carlin, U. S. A.* Page 8.

early in the Civil War.

Longstreet

Military Career

In 1849 while serving on the Texas frontier (following the Mexican-American War), George Pickett was promoted to first lieutenant; this was followed by promotion to captain in the Ninth U. S. Infantry in 1855.

Ironically, it was during his time on the Texas frontier that Pickett allegedly challenged future Union general Winfield Scott Hancock to a duel in 1853. According to the legend, Hancock declined the duel, and his supporters cited his refusal as the "respectable thing to do considering that duelling had by that time fallen out of social favor." While it might not be surprising that the native Virginian would challenge someone to a duel, and it wouldn't be surprising for a Pennsylvanian like Hancock to demur, this event has yet to be substantiated by a reputable source.

In 1856, Captain George Pickett transferred to the Northwest and served in the Washington Territory, where he commanded the construction of Fort Bellingham on Bellingham Bay in what is today the city of Bellingham, Washington. He also became involved in the dispute between the

U. S. and Great Britain over the boundary between Washington Territory and Canada in the San Juan Islands, an archipelago in the northwest corner of the contiguous United States between the U. S. mainland and Vancouver Island, British Columbia, Canada.

In 1859 Captain Pickett was dispatched in command of Company D, Ninth U. S. Infantry, to garrison San Juan Island in the northwest corner of the contiguous United States between the U. S. mainland and Vancouver Island, British Columbia, Canada, in response to dissonance that had erupted between American farmers and the Hudson's Bay Company. From 1859 to 1861, Pickett and his infantrymen would subsequently occupy one end of San Juan Island while the British held the other.

The confrontation was instigated when American farmer Lyman Cutler shot and killed a pig that had repeatedly broken into his garden. The pig belonged to the Hudson's Bay Company, and though Cutler was prepared to pay a fair price for the pig, the Company nevertheless insisted that Cutler face formal charges before a British magistrate. This touched off a territorial dispute that came to be derisively known as the "Pig War."

In response to occupation of the island by American forces, the British sent three warships and 1,000 men to force Pickett and his men off the island. Pickett defiantly refused the demand and instead ordered his men into a defensive line on the beach, exhorting them, "Don't be afraid of their big guns. We'll make a Bunker Hill of it!"[4] Ultimately, Pickett's defiance kept the British from landing, though he was certainly helped out by orders that the British were to avoid hostilities with American forces if possible. Thankfully, both sides proved unwilling to go to war over a pig.

The dispute at the heart of the "Pig War" lasted for three years, though no shots were fired on either side. Pickett's occupation of the contested land eventually led to an international agreement that placed San Juan Island within the United States territory.

Personal Life

In January 1851, First Lieutenant Pickett married Sally Harrison Minge. Sally hailed from a well-connected family in Virginia; she was the great-great-grandniece of President William Henry Harrison, and the great-great-granddaughter of Benjamin Harrison (a signer of the United States Declaration of Independence, not to be confused with the president of the same name). Tragically, Sally died during childbirth just 11 months after the couple married at Fort Gates, Texas. By some accounts, Sally went into labor during a Native American raid, and the child did not survive either. The infant daughter and wife were buried together.

---

[4] Robbins, James S. *Last in Their Class: Custer, Pickett and the Goats of West Point.* Page 177.

In 1856, while he was stationed in the Washington Territory and overseeing the construction of Fort Bellingham, Captain Pickett built a frame home that year that still stands today. In fact, the Pickett House remains the oldest house in Bellingham and the oldest house on its original foundation in the Pacific Northwest. While posted at Fort Bellingham, Pickett met and married a Native American woman of the Haida tribe named Princess Sakis Tiigang (Morning Mist), with whom he would have a son named James Tilton Pickett (born on December 31, 1857, but would die of tuberculosis at the age of thirty-two near Portland, Oregon in 1889). Morning Mist died a few months after giving birth to James.

The Pickett House

Thus, at just 33 years old, Captain Pickett had been married and left a widower twice, and he had a small son to consider. On top of that, Pickett's father died in December 1856 while Pickett was stationed at Fort Bellingham.

Chapter 4: Heading Toward War

Bleeding Kansas

While Pickett was on the frontier, thousands of miles away from the heartland, the United States was trying to sort out its intractable issues. In an attempt to organize the center of North America – Kansas and Nebraska – without offsetting the slave-free balance, Senator Stephen Douglas of Illinois proposed the Kansas-Nebraska Act. The Kansas-Nebraska Act eliminated the Missouri Compromise line of 1820, which the Compromise of 1850 had maintained. The Missouri Compromise had stipulated that states north of the boundary line determined in that bill would be free, and that states south of it *could* have slavery. This was essential to maintaining the balance of slave and free states in the Union. The Kansas-Nebraska Act, however, ignored the line completely and proposed that all new territories be organized by popular sovereignty. Settlers could vote whether they wanted their state to be slave or free.

Stephen Douglas, "The Little Giant"

When popular sovereignty became the standard in Kansas and Nebraska, the primary result was that thousands of zealous pro-slavery and anti-slavery advocates both moved to Kansas to influence the vote, creating a dangerous (and ultimately deadly) mix. Numerous attacks took place between the two sides, and many pro-slavery Missourians organized attacks on Kansas towns just across the border.

The best known abolitionist in Bleeding Kansas was a middle aged man named John Brown. A radical abolitionist, Brown organized a small band of like-minded followers and fought with the armed groups of pro-slavery men in Kansas for several months, including a notorious incident known as the Pottawatomie Massacre, in which Brown's supporters murdered five men. Over 50 people died before John Brown left the territory, which ultimately entered the Union as a free state in 1859.

John Brown

Harpers Ferry

After his activities in Kansas, John Brown spent the next few years raising money in New England, which would bring him into direct contact with important abolitionist leaders, including Frederick Douglass. Brown had previously organized a small raiding party that succeeded in raiding a Missouri farm and freeing 11 slaves, but he set his sights on far larger objectives. In 1859, Brown began to set a new plan in motion that he hoped would create a full scale slave uprising in the South. Brown's plan relied on raiding Harpers Ferry, a strategically located armory in western Virginia that had been the main federal arms depot after the Revolution. Given its proximity to the South, Brown hoped to seize thousands of rifles and move them south, gathering slaves and swelling his numbers as he went. The slaves would then be armed and ready to help free more slaves, inevitably fighting Southern militias along the way.

In recognition of how important escaped slave Frederick Douglass had become among abolitionists, Brown attempted to enlist the support of Douglass by informing him of the plans. While Douglass didn't blow the whistle on Brown, he told Brown that violence would only further enrage the South, and slaveholders might only retaliate further against slaves with devastating consequences. Instead of helping Brown, Douglass dissuaded freed blacks from joining Brown's group because he believed it was doomed to fail.

Despite that, in July 1859, Brown traveled to Harper's Ferry under an assumed name and waited for his recruits, but he struggled to get even 20 people to join him. Rather than call off the plan, however, Brown went ahead with it. That fall, Brown and his men used hundreds of rifles to seize the armory at Harper's Ferry, but the plan went haywire from the start, and word of his attack quickly spread. Local pro-slavery men formed a militia and pinned Brown and his men down while they were still at the armory.

After being called to Harpers Ferry, Robert E. Lee took decisive command of a troop of marines stationed there, surrounded the arsenal, and gave Brown the opportunity to surrender peaceably. When Brown refused, Lee ordered the doors be broken down and Brown taken captive, an affair that reportedly lasted just three minutes. A few of Brown's men were killed, but Brown was taken alive. Lee earned acclaim for accomplishing this task so quickly and efficiently.

Several of Pickett's future comrades in the Confederate Army of Northern Virginia were also at Harpers Ferry. Young JEB Stuart played an active role in opposing the raid at Harpers Ferry. In October of 1859, while conducting business in Washington, D.C., Stuart volunteered to carry secret instructions to Lieutenant Colonel Robert E. Lee and then accompany him and a squad of U. S. Military Militia to Harpers Ferry, where Brown had staged a raid on the armory. While delivering Lee's written ultimatum to the leader of the raid, who was going by the pseudonym Isaac Smith, Stuart remembered "Old Ossawatomie Brown" from the events at Bleeding Kansas, and ultimately assisted in his arrest.

The fallout from John Brown's raid on Harpers Ferry was intense. Southerners had long suspected that abolitionists hoped to arm the slaves and use violence to abolish slavery, and Brown's raid seemed to confirm that. Meanwhile, much of the northern press praised Brown for his actions. In the South, conspiracy theories ran wild about who had supported the raid, and many believed prominent abolitionist Republicans had been behind the raid as well. On the day of his execution, Brown wrote, "I, John Brown, am now quite *certain* that the crimes of this *guilty land* will never be purged away but with *blood.* I had, as I now think vainly, flattered myself that without very much bloodshed it might be done."

The man in command of the troops present at Brown's hanging was none other than Thomas Jonathan Jackson, who was ordered to Charlestown in November 1859. After Brown's hanging, the future Stonewall Jackson began to believe war was inevitable, but he wrote his aunt, "I think we have great reason for alarm, but my trust is in God; and I cannot think that He will permit the madness of men to interfere so materially with the Christian labors of this country at home and abroad."[5]

---

5   Davis, Burke. *They Called Him Stonewall: A Life of Lieutenant General T. J. Jackson, C. S. A.* Page 131.

Stonewall Jackson

The Election of 1860

In his memoirs, Pickett's future corps commander, General James Longstreet, summed up the national mood in the 1850s, likening it to a "war-cloud". "Officers of the Northern and Southern States were anxious to see the portending storm pass by or disperse, and on many occasions we, too, were assured, by those who claimed to look into the future, that the statesman would yet show himself equal to the occasion, and restore confidence among the people."

Clearly men like Longstreet were hoping at the time for some sort of grand compromise that would avert war, but by the Fall of 1860, everyone could see the "war-cloud" on the horizon. With the election of Republican candidate Abraham Lincoln as president on November 6, 1860, many Southerners considered it the final straw. Someone they knew as a "Black Republican", leader of a party whose central platform was to stop the spread of slavery to new states, was now set to be inaugurated as President in March.

Throughout the fall and winter of 1860, Southern calls for secession became increasingly serious. In a last-ditched effort to save the Union, Kentucky's Senator John Crittenden tried to assume the stateliness of his predecessor Henry Clay. Crittenden, however, proved to be no Henry Clay: his proposal that a Constitutional Amendment reinstate the Missouri Compromise line and extend it to the Pacific failed. President Buchanan supported the measure, but President-Elect Lincoln said he refused to allow the further expansion of slavery under any conditions.

The Crittenden Compromise failed on December 18. Two days later, South Carolina seceded from the Union. President Buchanan sat on his hands, believing the Southern states had no right to secede, but that the Federal government had no effective power to prevent secession. In January, Mississippi, Florida, Alabama, Georgia, Louisiana and Kansas followed South Carolina's lead. The Confederacy was formed on February 4th, in Montgomery, Alabama, with former Secretary of War Jefferson Davis as its President. On February 23rd, Texas joined the Confederacy.

Chapter 5: The Start of the Civil War

Lincoln had promised that it would not be the North that started a potential war, but he was also aware of the possibility of the South initiating conflict. Although he vowed not to fire the first shot, Lincoln was likely aware that his attempt to resupply Fort Sumter in Charleston Harbor would draw Southern fire; it had already happened under Buchanan's watch. After his inauguration, President Lincoln informed South Carolina governor Francis Pickens that he was sending supplies to the undermanned garrison at Fort Sumter. When Lincoln made clear that he would attempt to resupply the fort, Davis ordered Beauregard to demand its surrender and prevent the resupplying of the garrison.

In early April, the ship Lincoln sent to resupply the fort was fired upon and turned around. On April 9, Confederate President Davis sent word to General Beauregard to demand the fort's evacuation. At the time, the federal garrison consisted of Major Robert Anderson, Beauregard's artillery instructor from West Point, and 76 troops. Even before the bombardment, upon learning that he was opposed by Beauregard, Anderson remarked that the Southern forces in Charleston harbor would be exercised with "skill and sound judgment". Beauregard also remembered his former superior, and before the bombardment, he sent brandy, whiskey and cigars to Anderson and his garrison, gifts the Major refused.

At 4:30 a.m. on the morning of April 12, 1861, Beauregard ordered the first shots to be fired at Fort Sumter, effectively igniting the Civil War. After nearly 34 hours and thousands of rounds fired from 47 artillery guns and mortars ringing the harbor, on April 14, 1861, Major Anderson surrendered Fort Sumter, marking the first Confederate victory. No casualties were suffered on either side during the dueling bombardments across Charleston harbor, but, ironically, two Union soldiers were killed by an accidental explosion during the surrender ceremonies.

Beauregard

After the attack on Fort Sumter, support for both the northern and southern cause rose. Two days later, Lincoln issued a *call-to-arms* asking for 75,000 volunteers. That led to the secession of Virginia, Tennessee, North Carolina, and Arkansas, with the loyalty of border states like Kentucky, Maryland, and Missouri still somewhat up in the air. The large number of southern sympathizers in these states buoyed the Confederates' hopes that those too would soon join the South. Moreover, the loss of these border states, especially Virginia, all deeply depressed Lincoln. Just weeks before, prominent Virginians had reassured Lincoln that the state's historic place in American history made its citizens eager to save the Union. But as soon as Lincoln made any assertive moves to save the Union, Virginia seceded. This greatly concerned Lincoln, who worried Virginia's secession made it more likely other border states and/or Maryland would secede as well.

Despite the loss of Fort Sumter, the North expected a relatively quick victory. Their expectations weren't unrealistic, due to the Union's overwhelming economic advantages over the South. At the start of the war, the Union had a population of over 22 million. The South had a population of 9 million, nearly 4 million of whom were slaves. Union states contained 90% of the manufacturing capacity of the country and 97% of the weapon manufacturing capacity. Union states also possessed over 70% of the total railroads in the pre-war United States at the start of the war, and the Union also controlled 80% of the shipbuilding capacity of the pre-war United States.

Because of his ongoing responsibilities in the Washington Territory, Captain Pickett did not resign his U. S. Army commission and return to Virginia until two months after the firing on Fort Sumter. Despite the fact he abhorred slavery, Pickett's loyalty to Virginia trumped the federal government, so he traveled to Virginia, resigned his commission in the U.S. Army on June 25, 1861, and accepted a commission as a colonel in command of defenses at the Lower Rappahannock River Line of the Department of Fredericksburg, then under the command of Confederate Maj. General Theophilus H. Holmes. By January 14, 1862, Holmes had used his influence to have Pickett promoted to brigadier general.

Pickett later explained his thinking in a letter written to future wife Sallie Corbell:

No, my child, I had no conception of the intensity of feeling, the bitterness and hatred toward those who were so lately our friends and are now our enemies. I, of course, have always strenuously opposed disunion, not as doubting the right of secession, which was taught in our text-book at West Point, but as gravely questioning its expediency. I believed that the revolutionary spirit which infected both North and South was but a passing phase of fanaticism which would perish under the rebuke of all good citizens, who would surely unite in upholding the Constitution; but when that great assembly, composed of ministers, lawyers, judges, chancellors, statesmen, mostly white haired men of thought, met in South Carolina and when their districts were called crept noiselessly to the table in the center of the room and affixed their signatures to the parchment on which the ordinance of secession was inscribed, and when in deathly silence, spite of the gathered multitude, General Jamison arose and without preamble read: "The ordinance of secession has been signed and ratified; I proclaim the State of South Carolina an independent sovereignty," and lastly, when my old boyhood's friend called for an invasion, it was evident that both the advocates and opponents of secession had read the portents aright.

You know, my little lady, some of those cross-stitched mottoes on the cardboard samplers which used to hang on my nursery wall, such as, "He who provides not for his own household is worse than an infidel" and "Charity begins at home," made a lasting impression upon me; and while I love my neighbor, i.e., my country, I love my household, i. e., my state, more, and I could not be an infidel and lift my sword against my own kith and kin, even though I do believe, my most wise little counselor and confidante, that the measure of American greatness can be achieved only under one flag, and I fear, alas, there can never again reign for either of us the true spirit of national unity whether divided under two flags or united under one.

We did not tarry even for a day in 'Frisco, but under assumed names my friend, Sam

Barron, and I sailed for New York, where we arrived on the very day that Sam's father, Commodore Barron, was brought there a prisoner, which fact was proclaimed aloud by the pilot amid cheers of the passengers and upon our landing heralded by the newsboys with more cheers. Poor Sam had a hard fight to hide his feelings and to avoid arrest. We separated as mere ship acquaintances, and went by different routes to meet again, as arranged, at the house of Doctor Paxton, a Southern sympathizer and our friend.

On the next day we left for Canada by the earliest train. Thence we made our perilous way back south again, barely escaping arrest several times, and finally arrived in dear old Richmond, September 13th, just four days ago. I at once enlisted in the army and the following day was commissioned Captain. But so bitter is the feeling here that my being unavoidably delayed so long in avowing my allegiance to my state has been most cruelly and severely criticized by friends—yes, and even relatives, too.

Now, little one, if you had the very faintest idea how happy a certain captain in the C.S.A. (My, but that "C" looks queer!) would be to look into your beautiful, soul-speaking eyes and hear your wonderfully musical voice, I think you would let him know by wire where he could find you. I shall almost listen for the electricity which says, "I am at—. Come." I know that you will have mercy on your devoted

Those who didn't know Pickett from West Point or Mexico were in for quite a sight. Pickett cared quite a bit more for his martial appearance than the common soldier. Atop his thoroughbred "Old Black," Pickett cut quite a picture with a small blue kepi-style cap, buffed gloves over the sleeves of an immaculately tailored uniform that had a double row of gold buttons down the front of the coat, with a pair of shiny gold spurs on his highly polished boots. And whether mounted or walking, he made sure he was holding an elegant riding crop. His facial hair was always perfectly groomed, with his mustache turned upwards at the end, and his hair was described by one comrade as "long ringlets flowed loosely over his shoulders, trimmed and highly perfumed, his beard likewise was curling and giving up the scent of Araby."[6]

Chapter 6: The Peninsula Campaign

Planning for the Peninsula Campaign

Pickett's first combat command would come at the head of a brigade nicknamed the Gamecocks (part of Longstreet's division) during the Peninsula Campaign. After First Manassas, Joseph E. Johnston and his victorious Confederate army stayed camped near the outskirts of Washington D.C., while the North reorganized the Army of the Potomac under Pickett's friend George B. McClellan. McClellan was widely considered a prodigy for his West Point years, his

---

[6] Tagg, Larry. *The Generals of Gettysburg*. Pages 236—237.

service in Mexico, his observation during the Crimean War, and his oft-forgotten campaign in Western Virginia against Robert E. Lee in 1861. Though he is best known for his shortcomings today, McClellan had nearly ended Lee's Civil War career before it started, as General Lee was blamed throughout the South for losing western Virginia after his defeat at the Battle of Cheat Mountain. Lee would eventually be reassigned to constructing coastal defenses on the East Coast, and when his men dug trenches in preparation for the defense of Richmond, he was derisively dubbed the "King of Spades". That Lee was even in position to assume command of the Army of Northern Virginia the following year during the Peninsula Campaign was due more to his friendship with Jefferson Davis than anything else. The fact Davis played favorites with his generals crippled the South throughout the war, but it certainly worked in the South's favor with Lee.

As he was reorganizing the Army of the Potomac, McClellan vastly overestimated the strength of Johnston's army, leading him to plan an amphibious assault on Richmond that avoided Johnston's army in his front. In response, Johnston moved his army toward Culpeper Court House, which angered President Davis because it signified a retreat. For that reason, Davis brought Lee to Richmond as a military adviser, and he began to constrain Johnston's authority by issuing direct orders himself.

However, Johnston's movement had disrupted McClellan's anticipated landing spot. McClellan had already faced a number of issues in planning the campaign even before reaching the jumpoff point. The first option for the landing spot (Urbana) had been scrapped, and there was bickering over the amount of troops left around Washington without the Army of the Potomac fighting on the Overland line. Finally, in March of 1862, after nine months in command, General McClellan began his invasion of Virginia, initiating what would become known as the "Peninsula Campaign." Showing his proclivity for turning movement and grand strategy, McClellan completely shifted the theater of operations. Rather than march directly into Richmond and use his superior numbers to assert domination, he opted to exploit the Union sea dominance and move his army via an immense naval flotilla down the Potomac into Chesapeake Bay and land at Fort Monroe in Hampton, Virginia, at the southern tip of the Virginia Peninsula. In addition to his 130,000 thousand men, he moved 15,000 thousand horses and mules by boat as well. There he planned for an additional 80,000 men to join him, at which time he would advance westward to Richmond. One of the European observers likened the launch of the campaign to the "stride of a giant."

McClellan's Peninsula Campaign has been analyzed meticulously and is considered one of the grandest failures of the Union war effort, with McClellan made the scapegoat. In actuality, there was plenty of blame to go around, including Lincoln and his Administration, which was so concerned about Stonewall Jackson's army in the Shenandoah Valley that several Union armies were left in the Valley to defend Washington D.C., and even more were held back from

McClellan for fear of the capital's safety. The Administration also micromanaged the deployment of certain divisions, and with Stanton's decision to shut down recruiting stations in early 1862, combined with the Confederacy concentrating all their troops in the area, the Army of the Potomac was eventually outnumbered in front of Richmond.

At the beginning of the campaign, however, McClellan had vastly superior numbers at his disposal, with only about 70,000 Confederate troops on the entirety of the peninsula and fewer than 17,000 between him and Richmond. McClellan was unaware of this decisive advantage, however, because of the intelligence reports he kept receiving from Allen Pinkerton, which vastly overstated the number of available Confederate soldiers.

As Johnston marched his army to oppose McClellan, he was fully aware that he was severely outnumbered, even if McClellan didn't know that. For that reason, he was in constant communication with the leadership in Richmond, and in April he continued trying to persuade Davis and Lee that the best course of action would be to dig in and fight defensively around Richmond. President Davis would have none of it.

Yorktown

From the beginning, McClellan's caution and the narrow width of the Peninsula worked against his army. At Yorktown, which had been the site of a decisive siege during the Revolution, McClellan's initial hopes of surrounding and enveloping the Confederate lines through the use of the Navy was scuttled when the Navy couldn't promise that it'd be able to operate in the area. That allowed General John Magruder, whose Confederate forces were outmanned nearly 4-1, to hold Yorktown for the entire month of April. Magruder accomplished it by completely deceiving the federals, at times marching his men in circles to make McClellan think his army was many times larger. Other times, he spread his artillery batteries across the line and fired liberally and sporadically at the Union lines, just to give the impression that the Confederates had huge numbers. The ruse worked, leaving the Union command thinking there were 100,000 Confederates.

As a result of the misimpressions, McClellan chose not to attack Yorktown in force, instead opting to lay siege to it. In part, this was due to the decisive advantage the Union had in siege equipment, including massive mortars and artillery. The siege successfully captured Yorktown in early May with only about 500 casualties, but Magruder bought enough time for Johnston's army to confront McClellan on the Peninsula.

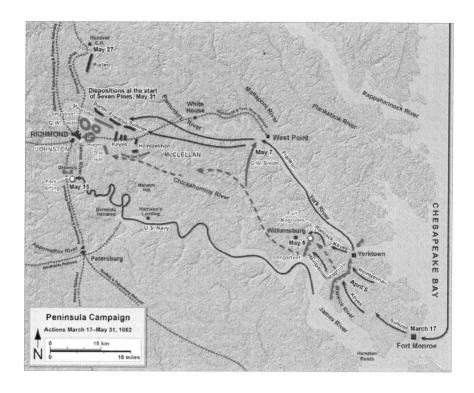

Williamsburg

   After withdrawing from Yorktown, McClellan sent Stoneman's cavalry in pursuit and attempted to move swiftly enough to cut off Johnston's retreat by use of Navy ships. At the battle of Williamsburg, which the Confederates fought as a delaying action to retreat, Pickett's brigade took part in some of the fighting that incurred 1600 casualties on the Confederates and 2200 upon the Union, but McClellan labeled it a "brilliant victory" over superior forces. Even then, the Union success was owed to Pickett's previous (alleged) antagonist, Brigadier General Winfield Scott Hancock, who had disregarded orders to withdraw from corps commander Sumner and repulsed a Confederate attack. For the action, which McClellan described as "superb", Hancock had earned his nickname "Hancock the Superb".

Hancock

The Battle of Seven Pines (Fair Oaks)

After Williamsburg, the Union army still had a nearly 2-1 advantage in manpower, so Johnston continued to gradually pull his troops back to a line of defense nearer Richmond as McClellan advanced. In conjunction, the U.S. Navy began moving its operations further up the James River, until it could get within 7 miles of the Confederate capital before being opposed by a Southern fort. McClellan continued to attempt to turn Johnston's flank, until the two armies were facing each other along the Chickahominy River. McClellan's Army of the Potomac got close enough to Richmond that they could see the city's church steeples.

By the end of May, Stonewall Jackson had startlingly defeated three separate Northern armies in the Valley, inducing Lincoln to hold back the I Corps from McClellan. When McClellan was forced to extend his line north to link up with troops that he expected to be sent overland to him, Johnston learned that McClellan was moving along the Chickahominy River. It was at this point that Johnston got uncharacteristically aggressive. Johnston had run out of breathing space for his army, and he believed McClellan was seeking to link up with McDowell's forces. Moreover, about a third of McClellan's army was south of the river, while the other parts of the army were still north of it, offering Johnston an enticing target. After a quick deluge turned the river into a rushing torrent that would make it impossible or the Union army to link back up or aid each other, Johnston drew up a very complex plan of attack for different wings of his army, and struck at the Army of the Potomac at the Battle of Seven Pines on May 31, 1862.

Like McDowell's plan for First Bull Run, the plan proved too complicated for Johnston's army to execute, and after a day of bloody fighting little was accomplished from a technical standpoint. At one point during the Battle of Seven Pines, Confederates in Longstreet's division marched in the wrong direction down the wrong road, causing congestion and confusion among other Confederate units and ultimately weakening the effectiveness of the massive Confederate counterattack launched against McClellan. Johnston wrote in his memoirs, "The operations of the Confederate troops in this battle were very much retarded by the dense woods and thickets that covered the ground, and by the deep mud and broad ponds of rain-water, in many places more than knee-deep, through which they had to struggle."

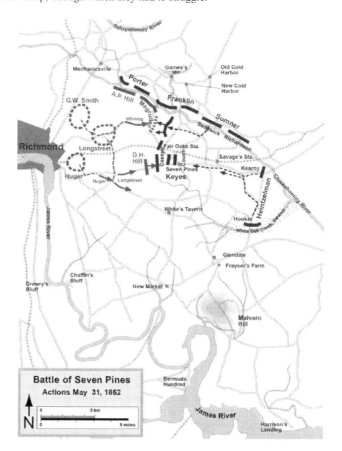

Pickett detailed his participation in a letter to Sallie Corbell:

Under orders from Old Peter [Longstreet], we marched at daylight and reported to D. H. Hill, near Seven Pines. Hill directed me to ride over and communicate with Hood. I started at once with Charlie and Archer, of my staff, to obey this order, but had gone only a short distance when we met a part of the Louisiana Zouaves in panic. I managed to seize and detain one fellow, mounted on a mule that seemed to have imbibed his rider's fear and haste. The man dropped his plunder and seizing his carbine threatened to kill me unless I released him at once, saying that the Yankees were upon his heels. We galloped back to Hill's headquarters—Archer bringing up the rear with the Zouave, who explained that the enemy were advancing in force and were within a few hundred yards of us. Hill ordered me to attack at once, which I did, driving them through an abatis over a crossroad leading to the railroad.

As we were nearing the second abatis, I, on foot at the time, noticed that Armistead's Brigade had broken, and sent a courier back post-haste to Hill for troops. A second and third message were sent and then a fourth, telling him that if he would send me more troops and ammunition we could drive the enemy across the Chickahominy. But alas, Hill, as brave, as great, as heroic a soldier as he is, has, since the fall of Johnston, been so bothered and annoyed with countermanding orders that he was, if I may say so, confused and failed to respond. After this delay nothing was left for us but to withdraw. Hill sent two regiments of Colston's Brigade and ordered Mahone's Brigade on my right, and at one o'clock at night, under his orders, we withdrew in perfect order and the enemy retreated to their bosky cover.

Thus, my darling, was ended the Battle of Seven Pines. No shot was fired afterward. How I wish I could say it ended all battles and that the last shot that will ever be heard was fired on June first, 1862. What a change love does make! How tender all things become to a heart touched by love—how beautiful the beautiful is and how abhorrent is evil! See, my darling, see what power you have— guard it well.

I have heard that my dear old friend, McClellan, is lying ill about ten miles from here. May some loving, soothing hand minister to him. He was, he is and he will always be, even were his pistol pointed at my heart, my dear, loved friend. May God bless him and spare his life. You, my darling, may not be in sympathy with this feeling, for I know you see "no good in Nazareth." Forgive me for feeling differently from you, little one, and please don't love me any the less. You cannot understand the entente cordiale between us "old fellows."

By the time the fighting was finished, nearly 40,000 had been engaged on both sides, and it was the biggest battle in the Eastern theater to date (second only to Shiloh at the time). However, McClellan was rattled by the attack, and near the end of the fighting that night Johnston had attempted to rally his men by riding up and down the battleline only to be nearly blown off his horse by artillery fire and having to be taken off the field. Johnston explained, "About seven o'clock I received a slight wound in the right shoulder from a musket-shot, and, a few moments after, was unhorsed by a heavy fragment of shell which struck my breast. Those around had me borne from the field in an ambulance; not, however, before the President, who was with General Lee, not far in the rear, had heard of the accident, and visited me, manifesting great concern, as he continued to do until I was out of danger." Having been seriously wounded, Johnston's command was given the following day to military advisor Robert E. Lee.

The Seven Days Battles

With more Confederate troops swelling the ranks, Lee's army was McClellan's equal by late June, and on June 25, Lee commenced an all-out attempt to destroy McClellan's army in a series of fierce battles known as the Seven Days Battles. After a stalemate in the first fighting at Oak Grove, Lee's army kept pushing ahead, using Stonewall Jackson to attack McClellan's right. Although Stonewall Jackson was unusually lethargic during the week's fighting, the appearance of his "foot cavalry" spooked McClellan even more, and McClellan was now certain he was opposed by 200,000 men, more than double the actual size of Lee's army. It also made McClellan think that the Confederates were threatening his supply line, forcing him to shift his army toward the James River to draw supplies.

On June 26, the Union defenders sharply repulsed the Confederate attacks at Mechanicsville, in part due to the fact that Stonewall Jackson had his troops bivouac for the night despite the fact heavy gunfire indicating a large battle was popping off within earshot.

The night before the Battle of Gaines' Mill, Pickett had a premonition that he wrote about the night before the battle:

"ALL last night, my darling Sally, the spirit of my dead mother seemed to hover over me. When she was living and I used to feel in that way, I always, as sure as fate, received from her a letter written at the very time that I had the sensation of her presence. I wonder if up there she is watching over me, trying to send me some message—some warning. I wish I knew.

This morning my brigade moved from its cantonments on the Williamsburg road and by daybreak was marching along the Mechanicsville turnpike, leading north of Richmond. The destination and character of the expedition, my darling, is unknown; but the position of other troops indicates a general movement. This evening we crossed the Chickahominy and are bivouacked on our guns in the road in front of Mechanicsville, from which point I am blessing my spirit and refreshing my soul by sending a message to my promised wife. I am tired and sleepy, several times to-day going to sleep on my horse.

This war was really never contemplated in earnest. I believe if either the North or the South had expected that their differences would result in this obstinate struggle, the cold-blooded Puritan and the cock hatted Huguenot and Cavalier would have made a compromise. Poor old Virginia came oftener than Noah's dove with her olive branch. Though she desired to be loyal to the Union of States, she did not believe in the right of coercion, and when called upon to furnish troops to restrain her sister states she refused, and would not even permit the passage of an armed force through her domain for that purpose. With no thought of cost, she rolled up her sleeves, ready to risk all in defense of a principle consecrated by the blood of her fathers. And now, alas, it is too late. We must carry through this bitter task unto the end. May the end be soon!"

Pickett finally had a chance to distinguish himself some more at Gaines' Mill, the third major fight of the Seven Days Battles. While leading an initial assault, Pickett was shot off his horse but continued to move forward with his men, leading his men and horse on foot. Brig. Eventually Pickett's brigade was repulsed and suffered losses as Confederate President Jefferson Davis himself looked on from behind the lines. Though the wound to his shoulder was not as critical as Pickett had initially thought, it proved severe enough that Pickett was out of action for the next three months, and he would subsequently miss the Second Battle of Bull Run and the Battle of Antietam while he recuperated.

While the Army of the Potomac kept retreating, McClellan managed to keep his forces in tact (mostly through the efforts of his field generals), ultimately retreating to Harrison's Landing on the James River and establishing a new base of operation. Feeling increasingly at odds with his superiors, in a letter sent from Gaines' Mills, Virginia dated June 28, 1862, a frustrated McClellan wrote to Secretary of War Stanton, "If I save the army now, I tell you plainly that I owe no thanks to any other person in the Washington. You have done your best to sacrifice this army."[7] McClellan's argument, however, flies in the face of common knowledge that he had become so obsessed with having sufficient supplies that he'd actually moved to Gaines' Mill to accommodate the massive amount of provisions he'd accumulated. Ultimately unable to move his cache of supplies as quickly as his men were needed, McClellan eventually ran railroad cars full of food and supplies into the Pamunkey River rather than leave them behind for the Confederates.

Despite the fact all of Lee's battle plans had been poorly executed by his generals, particularly Stonewall Jackson, he ordered one final assault against McClellan's army at Malvern Hill. Incredibly, McClellan was not even on the field for that battle, having left via steamboat back to Harrison's Landing. Biographer Ethan Rafuse notes McClellan's absence from the battlefield was inexcusable, literally leaving the Army of the Potomac leaderless during pitched battle, but McClellan often behaved coolly under fire, so it is likely not a question of McClellan's personal courage.

---

[7]   Lanning, Michael Lee. *The Civil War 100*. Page 189.

Ironically, Malvern Hill was one of the Union army's biggest successes during the Peninsula Campaign. Union artillery had silenced its Confederate counterparts, but Lee still ordered an infantry attack by D.H. Hill's division, which never got within 100 yards of the Union line. After the war, Hill famously referred to Malvern Hill, "It wasn't war. It was murder." Later that evening, as General Isaac Trimble (who is best known for leading a division during Pickett's Charge at Gettysburg) began moving his troops forward as if to attack, he was stopped by Stonewall Jackson, who asked "What are you going to do?" When Trimble replied that he was going to charge, Jackson countered, "General Hill has just tried with his entire division and been repulsed. I guess you'd better not try it."

Chapter 7: Returning to the Field

When Pickett returned to the action in September of 1862, he was given command of the two-brigade division in the corps commanded by his old colleague from Mexico, Maj. General James Longstreet, and subsequently promoted to major general on October 10, just two months before the Battle of Fredericksburg.

After McClellan failed to follow up to the Lincoln Administration's liking after Antietam, Lincoln appointed Ambrose Burnside, who had just failed at Antietam. Burnside didn't believe he was competent to command the entire army, a very honest (and accurate) judgment, but he also didn't want the command to fall upon Joe Hooker, who had been injured while aggressively fighting with his I Corps at Antietam. Thus, he accepted.

Under pressure from Lincoln to be aggressive, Burnside laid out a difficult plan to cross the Rappahannock and attack the Confederates near Fredericksburg. The plan was doomed from the very beginning. On December 12, Burnside's army struggled to cross the river under fire from Confederate sharpshooters in the town.

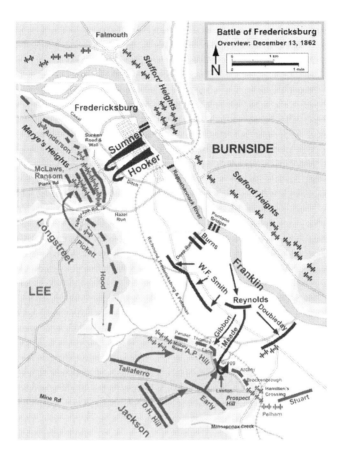

The majority of the fighting took place the next day, and the most contested fighting found Early and his men in the thick of it on the Confederates' right flank, which came under attack from General William B. Franklin. Franklin's "grand division" was able to penetrate General Jackson's defensive line to the south, but it was ultimately driven back by reinforcements.

However, the battle is mostly remembered for the piecemeal attacks the Union army made on heavily fortified positions Longstreet's men took up on Marye's Heights. With the massacre at Antietam still fresh in his mind (partially caused by the Confederates having not constructed defensive works), Longstreet ordered trenches, abatis (obstacles formed by felled trees with sharpened branches), and fieldworks to be constructed - which to Longstreet's credit, set a precedent for all future defensive battles of the Army of Northern Virginia. To his thinking, if the artillery didn't keep Union forces at bay, the twenty-five hundred Confederates lined up four-deep behind a quarter-mile long four-foot stone wall would deter even the most foolhardy. Thus when it was learned that General Burnside was planning a direct assault on "the Heights," even the other Union generals couldn't believe it.

Pickett and his men had been posted to the left of Jackson and to the right of Marye Heights, thus avoiding pitched battle for much of the day. As the Union assault against the Heights began in earnest, Pickett and his men were marched to the center of Longstreet's defensive line. As the Union soldiers threw themselves at Longstreet's heavily fortified position along the high ground, the Northern soldiers were mowed down again and again. General Longstreet compared the near continuous fall of soldiers on the battlefield to "the stead dripping of rain from the eaves of a house."[8] Still, Burnside sent wave after wave up the hill, with the Union injured (or those just cowering in the field) trying to stop the advancing men by grabbing at their legs and feet--begging them to turn back. In the end, a recorded 14 assaults were made on Marye's Heights, all of which failed, with over 12,650 Union soldiers killed, wounded, or gone missing. Despite all their efforts, not one Union soldier got within 100 feet of the wall at Marye's Heights before being shot or forced to withdraw.

As men lay dying on the field that night, the Northern Lights made a rare appearance. Southern soldiers took it as a divine omen and wrote about it frequently in their diaries. The Union soldiers saw less divine inspiration in the Northern Lights and mentioned it less in their own. The Battle of Fredericksburg also spawned one of Lee's most memorable quotes. During the battle, Lee turned to Longstreet and commented, "It is well that war is so terrible, otherwise we would grow too fond of it."[9]

After the virtual slaughter (with the dead said to have been stacked up in rows), the Union army retreated across the river in defeat. Although Lee had accomplished a decisive victory over Burnside's forces, the Union general had positioned his reserves and supply line so strategically that he could easily fall back without breaking lines of communication--while Lee had no such reserves or supplies. And since Lee didn't have the men to pursue and completely wipe out Burnside's army (and simply holding them would ultimately prove too costly), Lee chose not to give chase. Some military strategists contend this was a military blunder, but either way, the fighting in 1862 was done.

Pickett wrote in grandiose terms about Fredericksburg to Sallie:

---

[8]   Gaffney, P. and D. Gaffney. *The Civil War: Exploring History One Week at a Time.* Page 201

[9]   Nagel, Paul C. *The Lee's of Virginia.* Page 179.

"My division, nine thousand strong, is in fine shape. It was on the field of battle, as a division, for the first time yesterday, though only one brigade, Kemper's, was actively engaged. What a day it was, my darling—this ever to be remembered by many of us thirteenth of December—dawning auspiciously upon us clad in deepest, darkest mourning! A fog such as would shame London lay over the valley, and through the dense mist distinctly came the uncanny commands of the unseen opposing officers. My men were eager to be in the midst of the fight, and if Hood had not been so cautious they would probably have immortalized themselves. Old Peter's orders were that Hood and myself were to hold our ground of defense unless we should see an opportunity to attack the enemy while engaged with A. P. Hill on the right. A little after ten, when the fog had lifted and Stuart's cannon from the plain of Massaponax were turned upon Meade and when Franklin's advance left the enemy's flank open, I went up to Hood and urged him to seize the opportunity; but he was afraid to assume so great a responsibility and sent for permission to Old Peter, who was with Marse Robert in a different part of the field. Before his assent and approval were received, the opportunity, alas, was lost!

If war, my darling, is a necessity—and I suppose it is—it is a very cruel one. Your Soldier's heart almost stood still as he watched those sons of Erin fearlessly rush to their death. The brilliant assault on Marye's Heights of their Irish Brigade was beyond description. Why, my darling, we forgot they were fighting us, and cheer after cheer at their fearlessness went up all along our lines. About fifty of my division sleep their last sleep at the foot of Marye's Heights.

I can't help feeling sorry for Old Burnside - proud, plucky, hard-headed old dog. I always liked him, but I loved little Mac, 1 and it was a godsend to the Confederacy that he was relieved.

Oh, my darling, war and its results did not seem so awful till the love for you came. Now—now I want to love and bless and help everything, and there are no foes—no enemies just love for you and longing for you."

After the battle, Pickett's division remained part of General Longstreet's corps and spent most of the spring of 1863 in southeastern Virginia, refitting and gathering supplies for the next campaign.

Chancellorsville

After the Confederate victory at Fredericksburg, Lee dispatched Longstreet and his corps back to the Virginia Peninsula to protect Richmond and gather food and other much-needed supplies. Although Longstreet accomplished both missions, he was later criticized for having not taken advantage of the opportunity to attack Union positions in the area. As had now become Longstreet's *modus operandi*, to deflect responsibility, he simply responded that he didn't think they could afford the "powder and ball"--an assertion many historians fully doubt.

In May of 1863, General Lee ordered Longstreet to rejoin his Army of Northern Virginia in time for a potential battle, which would come at the very beginning of May. Longstreet's men would not reach Chancellorsville in time, but it still ended up being a stunning victory for the Confederates.

Lee had concluded an incredibly successful year for the Confederates in the East, but the South was still struggling. The Confederate forces in the West had failed to win a major battle, suffering defeat at places like Shiloh in Tennessee and across the Mississippi River. As the war continued into 1863, the southern economy continued to deteriorate. Southern armies were suffering serious deficiencies of nearly all supplies as the Union blockade continued to be effective as stopping most international commerce with the Confederacy. Moreover, the prospect of Great Britain or France recognizing the Confederacy had been all but eliminated by the Emancipation Proclamation.

Given the unlikelihood of forcing the North's capitulation, the Confederacy's main hope for victory was to win some decisive victory or hope that Abraham Lincoln would lose his reelection bid in 1864, and that the new president would want to negotiate peace with the Confederacy. Understandably, this colored Confederate war strategy, and unquestionably Lee's.

After the Fredericksburg debacle and the "Mud March" fiasco that left a Union advance literally dead in its tracks, Lincoln fired Burnside and replaced him with "Fighting Joe" Hooker. Hooker had gotten his nickname from a clerical error in a newspaper's description of fighting, but the nickname stuck, and Lee would later playfully refer to him as F.J. Hooker. Hooker had stood out for his zealous fighting at Antietam, and the battle may very well have turned out differently if he hadn't been injured at the head of the I Corps. Now he was in command of a 100,000 man Army of the Potomac, and he devised a complex plan to cross the Rappahannock River with part of his force near Fredericksburg to pin down Lee while using the other bulk to turn Lee's left, which would allow his forces to reach the Confederate rear.

Hooker's plan initially worked perfectly, with the division of his army surprising Lee. Lee was outnumbered two to one and now had to worry about threats on two fronts. Incredibly, Lee once again decided to divide his forces in the face of the enemy, sending Stonewall Jackson to turn the Union army's right flank while the rest of the army maintained positions near Fredericksburg. The Battle of Chancellorsville is one of the most famous of the Civil War, and the most famous part of the battle was Stonewall Jackson's daring march across the Army of the Potomac's flank, surprising the XI Corps with an attack on May 2, 1863. Having ignored warnings of Jackson's march, the XI Corps was quickly routed.

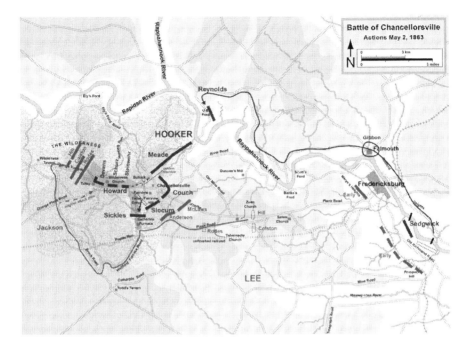

The surprise was a costly success however. Jackson scouted out ahead of his lines later that night and was mistakenly fired upon by his own men, badly wounding him. Jackson's natural replacement, A.P. Hill, was also injured, so Lee had cavalry leader J.E.B. Stuart assume command of Jackson's corps with Jackson out of action. On May 3, Stuart fiercely attacked the Union army, attempting to push them into the river, while on the other flank, the Confederates evacuated from Fredericksburg but ultimately held the line. Hooker began to lose his nerve, and he was injured during the battle when a cannonball nearly killed him. Historians now believe that Hooker may have commanded part of the battle while suffering from a concussion.

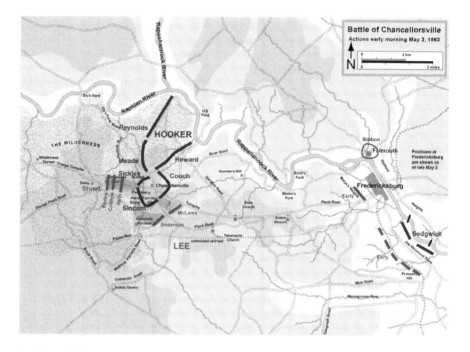

By the end of the battle, the Army of the Potomac had once again been defeated, retreating across the river. But Lee would also lose his "right hand". After Jackson's left arm was amputated, he seemed to be recovering, but his doctors were unaware of his symptoms that indicated oncoming pneumonia. Jackson would die May 10, eight days after his brilliant attack.

Chapter 8: The Heart of a Soldier

Before the battle that would make his name immortal, Pickett met a young girl named Sallie Corbell, who would go on to become responsible for much of Pickett's legacy. It was Sallie who later published extensively about Pickett's life, spreading some of the legends associated with Pickett today.

Sallie claimed that she had first met Pickett several years before Gettysburg, when she was still a teenager. In *The Heart of a Soldier, as Revealed in the Intimate Letters of General George E. Pickett C.S.A.*, Sallie wrote of her first encounter with her future husband:

"EARLY in life's morning I knew and loved him, and from my first meeting with him to the end, I always called him "Soldier"—"My Soldier." I was a wee bit of a girl at that first meeting. I had been visiting my grandmother, when whooping-cough broke out in the neighborhood, and she took me off to Old Point Comfort to visit her friend, Mrs. Boykin, the sister of John Y. Mason. I could dance and sing and play games and was made much of by the other children and their parents there, till I suddenly developed the cough, then I was shunned and isolated.

I could not understand the change. I would press my face against the ball-room window-panes and watch the merry-making inside and my little heart would almost break. One morning, while playing alone on the beach, I saw an officer lying on the sand reading, under the shelter of an umbrella. I had noticed him several times, always apart from the others, and very sad. I could imagine but one reason for his desolation and in pity for him, I crept under his umbrella to ask him if he, too, had the whooping-cough. He smiled and answered no; but as I still persisted he drew me to him, telling me that he had lost someone who was dear to him and he was very lonely.

And straightway, without so much as a by-your-leave, I promised to take the place of his dear one and to comfort him in his loss. Child as I was, I believe I lost my heart to him on the spot. At all events, I crept from under the umbrella pledged to Lieutenant George E. Pickett, U. S. A., for life and death, and I still hold most sacred a little ring and locket that he gave me on that day.

It is small wonder that this first picture of him is among the most vivid still; the memory of him as he lay stretched in the shade of the umbrella, not tall, and rather slender, but very graceful, and perfect in manly beauty. With childish appreciation, I particularly noticed his very small hands and feet. He had beautiful gray eyes that looked at me through sunny lights—eyes that smiled with his lips. His mustache was gallantly curled. His hair was exactly the color of mine, dark brown, and long and wavy, in the fashion of the time. The neatness of his dress attracted even a child's admiration. His shirt-front of the finest white linen, was in soft puffs and ruffles, and the sleeves were edged with hem-stitched thread cambric ruffles. He would never, to the end of his life, wear the stiff linen collars and cuffs and stocks which came into fashion among men. While he was at West Point he paid heavily in demerits for obstinacy in refusing to wear the regulation stock. Only when the demerits reached the danger-point would he temporarily give up his soft necktie.

It was under that umbrella, in the days that followed, that I learned, while he guided my hand, to make my first letters and spell my first words. They were "Sally" and "Soldier." I remember, too, the songs he used to sing me in the clear, rich voice of which his soldiers were so fond, frequently accompanying himself on the guitar. He kept a diary of those days and after the war it was returned to him from San Juan by the British officer who occupied the island conjointly with him before the opening of the war. I have it now in my possession."

Although Sallie would later write that she met George in 1852 (when she was nine years of age), records indicate that she did not marry the thirty-eight-year-old widower until November 13, 1863, when she was twenty. George and Sallie would have two sons together, George Jr. and Corbell.

Historians further dispute Sallie's claim that she met George at Old Point Comfort (Hampton, Virginia) when she was still a child, as stated in her books. In a letter written by Pickett himself dated August 28, 1863, he refers to John D. Corbell, Sallie's father, as "never having seen me," and in a letter Pickett wrote to Sallie in 1864 he refers to having met two miles of *this* place-- within a half mile of Chester. Chester is actually about 100 miles from Old Point Comfort.

Pickett would continue to write to her, and it was his letters to her during the Pennsylvania Campaign that are the only surviving personal accounts about the campaign written by the general.

Chapter 9: Invading Pennsylvania

Heading Towards Gettysburg

In the spring of 1863, General Lee discovered that McClellan had known of his plans and was able to force a battle at Antietam before all of General Lee's forces had arrived. General Lee now believed that he could successfully invade the North again, and that his defeat before was due in great measure to a stroke of bad luck. In addition, General Lee hoped to supply his army on the unscathed fields and towns of the North, while giving war ravaged northern Virginia a rest. After Chancellorsville, Longstreet and Lee met to discuss options for the Confederate Army's summer campaign. Longstreet advocated detachment of all or part of his corps to be sent to Tennessee, citing Union Maj. General Ulysses S. Grant's advance on Vicksburg, the critical Confederate stronghold on the Mississippi River. Longstreet argued that a reinforced army under Bragg could defeat Rosecrans and drive toward the Ohio River, compelling Grant to release his hold on Vicksburg. Lee, however, was opposed to a division of his army and instead advocated a large-scale offensive (and raid) into Pennsylvania. In addition, General Lee hoped to supply his army on the unscathed fields and towns of the North, while giving war ravaged northern Virginia a rest.

Knowing that victories on Virginia soil meant little to an enemy that could simply retreat, regroup, and then return with more men and more advanced equipment, Lee set his sights on a Northern invasion, aiming to turn Northern opinion against the war and against President Lincoln. With his men already half-starved from dwindling provisions, Lee intended to confiscate food, horses, and equipment as they pushed north--and hopefully influence Northern politicians into giving up their support of the war by penetrating into Harrisburg or even

Philadelphia. Given the right circumstances, Lee's army might even be able to capture either Baltimore or Philadelphia and use the city as leverage in peace negotiations.

In the wake of Jackson's death, Lee reorganized his army, creating three Corps out of the previous two, with A.P. Hill and Richard S. Ewell "replacing" Stonewall. Hill had been a successful division commander, but he was constantly battling bouts of sickness that left him disabled, which would occur at Gettysburg. Ewell had distinguished himself during the Peninsula Campaign, suffering a serious injury that historians often credit as making him more cautious in command upon his return.

Pickett wrote home to Sallie just a week before the battle to mention a humorous anecdote:

"Yesterday my men were marching victoriously through the little town of Greencastle, the bands all playing our glorious, soul inspiring, southern airs: "The Bonny Blue Flag," "My Maryland," "Her Bright Smile Haunts Me Still," and the soldiers all happy, hopeful, joyously keeping time to the music, many following it with their voices and making up for the want of the welcome they were not receiving in the enemy's country by cheering themselves and giving themselves a welcome. As Floweree's band, playing "Dixie," was passing a vine-bowered home, a young girl rushed out on the porch and waved a United States flag. Then, either fearing that it might be taken from her or finding it too large and unwieldy, she fastened it around her as an apron, and taking hold of it on each side and waving it in defiance, called out with all the strength of her girlish voice and all the courage of her brave young heart:

"Traitors—traitors—traitors, come and take this flag, the man of you who dares!"

Knowing that many of my men were from a section of the country which had been within the enemy's lines, and fearing lest some might forget their manhood, I took off my hat and bowed to her, saluted her flag and then turned, facing the men who felt and saw my unspoken order. And don't you know that they were all Virginians and didn't forget it, and that almost every man lifted his cap and cheered the little maiden who, though she kept on waving her flag, ceased calling us traitors, till letting it drop in front of her she cried out:

"Oh, I wish I wish I had a rebel flag; I'd wave that, too."

The picture of that little girl in the vine-covered porch, beneath the purple morning glories with their closed lips and bowed heads waiting and saving their prettiness and bloom for the coming morn—of course, I thought of you, my darling. For the time, that little Greencastle Yankee girl with her beloved flag was my own little promised-to-be-wife, receiving from her Soldier and her Soldier's soldiers the reverence and homage due her.

We left the little girl standing there with the flag gathered up in her arms, as if too sacred to be waved now that even the enemy had done it reverence."

Stuart's Ride

JEB Stuart

During the first weeks of summer of 1863, as JEB Stuart screened the army and completed several well-executed offenses against Union cavalry, many historians think it likely that he had already planned to remove the negative effect of Brandy Station by duplicating one of his now famous circumnavigating rides around the enemy army. But as Lee began his march north through the Shenandoah Valley in western Virginia, it is highly unlikely that is what he wanted or expected.

Before setting out on June 22, the methodical Lee gave Stuart specific instructions as to the role he was to play in the Pennsylvania offensive: as the "Eyes of the Army" he was to guard the mountain passes with part of his force while the Army of Northern Virginia was still south of the Potomac River, and then cross the river with the remainder of his army and screen the right flank of Confederate general Richard Ewell's Second Corps as it moved down the Shenandoah Valley, maintaining contact with Ewell's army as it advanced towards Harrisburg.

But instead of taking the most direct route north near the Blue Ridge Mountains, Stuart chose a much more ambitious course of action. Stuart decided to march his three best brigades (under

Generals Hampton and Fitzhugh Lee, and Col. John R. Chambliss) between the Union army and Washington, north through Rockville to Westminster, and then into Pennsylvania--a route that would allow them to capture supplies along the way and wreak havoc as they skirted Washington. In the aftermath, the *Washington Star* would write: "The cavalry chief [Stuart] interpreted his marching orders in a way that best suited his nature, and detached his 9000 troopers from their task of screening the main army and keeping tabs on the Federals. When Lee was in Pennsylvania anxiously looking for him, Stuart crossed the Potomac above Washington and captured a fine prize of Federal supply wagons . . . ."[10]

But to complicate matters even more, as Stuart set out on June 25 on what was probably a glory-seeking mission, he was unaware that his intended path was blocked by columns of Union infantry that would invariably force him to veer farther east than he or Lee had anticipated. Ultimately, his decision would prevent him from linking up with Ewell as ordered and deprive Lee of his primary cavalry force as he advanced deeper and deeper into unfamiliar enemy territory. According to Halsey Wigfall (son of Confederate States Senator Louis Wigfall) who was in Stuart's infantry, "Stuart and his cavalry left [Lee's] army on June 24 and did not contact [his] army again until the afternoon of July 2, the second day of the [Gettysburg] battle."[11]

According to Stuart's own account, on June 29 his men clashed briefly with two companies of Union cavalry in Westminster, Maryland, overwhelming and chasing them "a long distance on the Baltimore road," causing a "great panic" in the city of Baltimore. On June 30, the head of Stuart's column then encountered Union Brig. General Judson Kilpatrick's cavalry as it passed through Hanover--reportedly capturing a wagon train and scattering the Union army--after which Kilpatrick's men were able to regroup and drive Stuart and his men out of town. Then after a twenty-mile trek in the dark, Stuart's exhausted men reached Dover, Pennsylvania, on the morning of July 1 (which they briefly occupied).

Given great discretion in his cavalry operations before the battle, Stuart's cavalry was too far removed from the Army of Northern Virginia to warn Lee of the Army of the Potomac's movements. As it would turn out, Lee's army inadvertently stumbled into Union cavalry and then the Union army at Gettysburg on the morning of July 1, 1863, walking blindly into what became the largest battle of the war.

Late on the second day of the battle, Stuart finally arrived, bringing with him the caravan of captured Union supply wagons, and he was immediately reprimanded by Lee. One account describes Lee as "visibly angry" raising his hand "as if to strike the tardy cavalry commander."[12]

---

[10]   Stepp, John W. & Hill, William I. (editors), *Mirror of War, the Washington Star reports the Civil War*. Page 199.
[11]   Eaton, Clement. *Jefferson Davis*. Page 178.
[12]   Philips, David. *Crucial Land Battles*. Page 75.

While that does not sound like Lee's style, Stuart has been heavily criticized ever since, and it has been speculated Lee took him to task harshly enough that Stuart offered his resignation. Lee didn't accept it, but he would later note in his after battle report that the cavalry had not updated him as to the Army of the Potomac's movements.

On June 25, 1863, Confederate General Richard Ewell, positioned at Chambersburg in South-Central Pennsylvania, divided his corps, assigning Major General Early to lead one division to York *via* Gettysburg. Ransacking York on June 28 (as well as destroying a ten-mile section of the Northern Central railroad), Early intended to proceed to Harrisburg but when he reached the bridge spanning the Susquehanna River, he discovered that it had been burned by a Union detachment. The following day, Ewell received word from General Lee to converge on Cashtown, Pennsylvania and await the remainder of the Army of Northern Virginia.

Chapter 10: July 1, 1863

It is believed that one of the first notices Lee got about the Army of the Potomac's movements actually came from a spy named "Harrison", a man who apparently worked undercover for Longstreet but of whom little is known. Harrison reported that General George G. Meade was now in command of the Union Army and was at that very moment marching north to meet Lee's army. According to Longstreet, he and Lee were supposedly on the same page at the beginning of the campaign. "His plan or wishes announced, it became useless and improper to offer suggestions leading to a different course. All that I could ask was that the policy of the campaign should be one of defensive tactics; that we should work so as to force the enemy to attack us, in such good position as we might find in our own country, so well adapted to that purpose—which might assure us of a grand triumph. To this he readily assented as an important and material adjunct to his general plan." Lee later claimed he "had never made any such promise, and had never thought of doing any such thing," but in his official report after the battle, Lee also noted, "It had not been intended to fight a general battle at such a distance from our base, unless attacked by the enemy.

Without question, the most famous battle of the Civil War took place outside of the small town of Gettysburg, Pennsylvania, which happened to be a transportation hub, serving as the center of a wheel with several roads leading out to other Pennsylvanian towns. Lee was unaware of Meade's position when an advanced division of Hill's Corps marched toward Gettysburg on the morning of July 1.

The battle began with John Buford's Union cavalry forces skirmishing against the advancing division of Heth's just outside of town. Buford intentionally fought a delaying action that was meant to allow John Reynolds' I Corps to reach Gettysburg and engage the Confederates, which eventually set the stage for a general battle.

The I Corps was led by Pennsylvanian General John F. Reynolds, an effective general that had been considered for command of the entire army in place of Hooker and was considered by many the best general in the army. Since Lee had invaded Pennsylvania, many believe that Reynolds was even more active and aggressive than he might have otherwise been. In any event, Reynolds was personally at the front positioning two brigades, exhorting his men, "Forward men! Forward for God's sake, and drive those fellows out of the woods."

As he was at the front positioning his men, Reynolds fell from his horse, having been hit by a bullet behind the ear that killed him almost instantly. With his death, command of the I Corps fell upon Maj. Gen. Abner Doubleday, the Civil War veteran wrongly credited for inventing baseball. Despite the death of the corps commander, the I Corps successfully managed to drive the Confederates in their sector back, highlighted by sharp fighting from the Iron Brigade, a brigade comprised of Wisconsin, Indiana, and Michigan soldiers from the "West". In an unfinished railroad cut, the 6th Wisconsin captured the 2nd Mississippi, and regimental commander Rufus Dawes reported, "The officer replied not a word, but promptly handed me his sword, and his men, who still held them, threw down their muskets. The coolness, self possession, and discipline which held back our men from pouring a general volley saved a hundred lives of the enemy, and as my mind goes back to the fearful excitement of the moment, I marvel at it."

Around noon, the battle hit a lull, in part because Confederate division commander Henry Heth was under orders to avoid a general battle in the absence of the rest of the Army of Northern Virginia. At that point, however, the Union had gotten the better of the fighting, and the Confederate army was concentrating on the area, with more soldiers in Hill's corps in the immediate vicinity and Ewell's corps marching from the north toward the town.

As the Union's I Corps held the line, General Oliver O. Howard and his XI Corps came up on the right of the I Corps, eager to replace the stain the XI Corps had suffered at Chancellorsville thanks to Stonewall Jackson. As a general battle began to form northwest of town, news was making its way back to Meade several miles away that Reynolds had been killed, and that a battle was developing.

Meade had been drawing up a proposed defensive line several miles away from Gettysburg near Emmitsburg, Maryland, but when news of the morning's fighting reached him, Meade sent II Corps commander Winfield Scott Hancock ahead to take command in the field, putting him in temporary command of the "left wing" of the army consisting of the I, II, III and XI Corps. Meade also charged Hancock with determining whether to fight the general battle near Gettysburg or to pull back to the line Meade had been drawing up. Hancock would not be the senior officer on the field (Oliver Howard outranked him), so the fact that he was ordered to take command of the field demonstrates how much Meade trusted him.

As Hancock headed toward the fighting, and while the Army of the Potomac's I and XI Corps engaged in heavy fighting, they were eventually flanked from the north by Early's division, which was returning toward Gettysburg from its previous objective. For the XI Corps, it was certainly reminiscent of their retreat at Chancellorsville, and they began a disorderly retreat through the streets of the small town. Fighting broke out in various places throughout the town, while some Union soldiers hid in and around houses for the duration of the battle. Gettysburg's citizens also fled in the chaos and fighting.

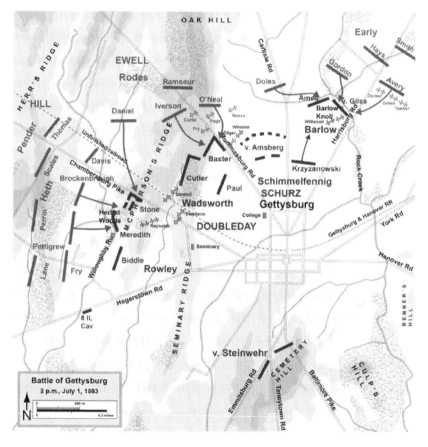

After a disorderly retreat through the town itself, the Union men began to dig in on high ground to the southeast of the town. When Hancock met up with Howard, the two briefly argued over the leadership arrangement, until Howard finally acquiesced. Hancock told the XI Corps commander, "I think this the strongest position by nature upon which to fight a battle that I ever saw." When Howard agreed, Hancock replied, "Very well, sir, I select this as the battle-field."

As the Confederates sent the Union corps retreating, Lee arrived on the field and saw the importance of the defensive positions the Union men were taking up along Cemetery Hill and Culp's Hill. Late in the afternoon, Lee sent discretionary orders to Ewell that Cemetery Hill be taken "if practicable", but ultimately Ewell chose not to attempt the assault. Lee's order has been criticized because it left too much discretion to Ewell, leaving historians to speculate on how the more aggressive Stonewall Jackson would have acted on this order if he had lived to command this wing of Lee's army, and how differently the second day of battle would have proceeded with Confederate possession of Culp's Hill or Cemetery Hill. Discretionary orders were customary for General Lee because Jackson and Longstreet, his other principal subordinate, usually reacted to them aggressively and used their initiative to act quickly and forcefully. Ewell's decision not to attack, whether justified or not, may have ultimately cost the Confederates the battle. Edwin Coddington, widely considered the historian who wrote the greatest history of the battle, concluded, "Responsibility for the failure of the Confederates to make an all-out assault on Cemetery Hill on July 1 must rest with Lee. If Ewell had been a Jackson he might have been able to regroup his forces quickly enough to attack within an hour after the Yankees had started to retreat through the town. The likelihood of success decreased rapidly after that time unless Lee were willing to risk everything."

With so many men engaged and now taking refuge on the high ground, Meade, who was an engineer like Lee, abandoned his previous plan to draw up a defensive line around Emmittsburg a few miles to the south. After a council of war, the Army of the Potomac decided to defend at Gettysburg.

Day 1 by itself would have been one of the 25 biggest battles of the Civil War, and it was a tactical Confederate victory. Union casualties were almost 9,000, and the Confederates suffered slightly more than 6,000. But the battle had just started, and thanks to the actions of Meade and Hancock, the largest battle on the North American continent would take place on the ground of their choosing.

As the other corps of Lee's army were engaged, Longstreet's corps did not fight during the first day. Pickett's division was at Chambersburg, detached from the other two divisions of Longstreet's corps at Greenwood, about seven miles to the east. All three divisions were waiting for orders to march over South Mountain toward the battle that was already raging about twenty miles away, but Pickett's division, guarding the Confederate Army's rear, was ordered to remain in Chambersburg until relieved by cavalry general John Daniel Imboden's brigade (which was behind schedule in arriving). Thus, Pickett's men didn't receive orders to advance toward

Gettysburg until the night of July 1.

Chapter 11: July 2, 1863

By the morning of July 2, Major General Meade had put in place what he thought to be the optimal battle strategy. Positioning his now massive Army of the Potomac in what would become known as the "fish hook", he'd established a line configuration that was much more compact and maneuverable than Lee's, which allowed Meade to shift his troops quickly from inactive parts of the line to those under attack without creating new points of vulnerability. Moreover, Meade's army was taking a defensive stance on the high ground anchored by Culp's Hill, Cemetery Hill, and Cemetery Ridge. Meade also personally moved the III Corps under Maj. General Daniel Sickles into position on the left of the line.

On the morning of July 2, Meade was determined to make a stand at Gettysburg, and Lee was determined to strike at him. That morning, Lee decided to make strong attacks on both Union flanks while feinting in the middle, ordering Ewell's corps to attack Culp's Hill on the Union right while Longstreet's corps would attack on the Union left. Lee hoped to seize Cemetery Hill, which would give the Confederates the high ground to harass the Union supply lines and command the road to Washington, D.C. Lee also believed that the best way to do so would be to use Longstreet's corps to launch an attack up the Emmitsburg Road, which he figured would roll up the Union's left flank, presumed to be on Cemetery Hill. Lee was mistaken, due in part to the fact Stuart and his cavalry couldn't perform reconnaissance. In fact, the Union line extended farther south than Cemetery Hill, with the II Corps positioned on Cemetery Ridge and the III Corps nearly as far south as the base of Little Round Top and Round Top. Moreover, Ewell protested that this battle plan would demoralize his men, since they'd be forced to give up the ground they had captured the day before.

As it turned out, both attacks ordered by Lee would come too late. Though there was a controversy over when Lee ordered Longstreet's attack, Longstreet's march got tangled up and caused several hours of delay. Lost Cause advocates attacking Longstreet would later claim his attack was supposed to take place as early as possible, although no official Confederate orders gave a time for the attack. Lee gave the order for the attack around 11:00 a.m., and it is known that Longstreet was reluctant about making it; he still wanted to slide around the Union flank, interpose the Confederate army between Washington D.C. and the Army of the Potomac, and force Meade to attack them. Between Longstreet's delays and the mixup in the march that forced parts of his corps to double back and make a winding march, Longstreet's men weren't ready to attack until about 4:00 p.m.

Longstreet's biographer, Jeffrey Wert, wrote, "Longstreet deserves censure for his performance on the morning of July 2. He allowed his disagreement with Lee's decision to affect his conduct.

Once the commanding general determined to assail the enemy, duty required Longstreet to comply with the vigor and thoroughness that had previously characterized his generalship. The concern for detail, the regard for timely information, and the need for preparation were absent." Edwin Coddington, whose history of the Gettysburg Campaign still continues to be considered the best ever written, described Longstreet's march as "a comedy of errors such as one might expect of inexperienced commanders and raw militia, but not of Lee's ' War Horse' and his veteran troops." Coddington considered it "a dark moment in Longstreet's career as a general."

Writing about July 2, Longstreet criticized Lee, insisting once again that the right move was to move around the Union flank. "The opportunity for our right was in the air. General Halleck saw it from Washington. General Meade saw and was apprehensive of it. Even General Pendleton refers to it in favorable mention in his official report. Failing to adopt it, General Lee should have gone with us to his right. He had seen and carefully examined the left of his line, and only gave us a guide to show the way to the right, leaving the battle to be adjusted to formidable and difficult grounds without his assistance. If he had been with us, General Hood's messengers could have been referred to general Headquarters, but to delay and send messengers five miles in favor of a move that he had rejected would have been contumacious. The opportunity was with the Confederates from the assembling on Cemetery Hill. It was inviting of their preconceived plans. It was the object of and excuse for the invasion as a substitute for more direct efforts for the relief of Vicksburg. Confederate writers and talkers claim that General Meade could have escaped without making aggressive battle, but that is equivalent to confession of the inertia that failed to grasp the opportunity."

As Longstreet's men began their circuitous march, Union III Corps commander Dan Sickles took it upon himself to advance his entire corps one half mile forward to a peach orchard, poising himself to take control of higher ground. Some historians assert that Sickles had held a grudge against Meade for taking command from his friend Joseph Hooker and intentionally disregarded orders. It has also been speculated by some historians that Sickles moved forward to occupy high ground in his front due to the devastation unleashed against the III Corps at Chancellorsville once Confederates took high ground and operated their artillery on Hazel Grove. Sickles and Meade would feud over the actions on Day 2 in the years after the war, after Sickles (who lost a leg that day) took credit for the victory by disrupting Lee's attack plans. Historians have almost universally sided with Meade, pointing out that Sickles nearly had his III Corps annihilated during Longstreet's attack.

Whatever the reasoning for Sickles' move, this unauthorized action completely undermined Meade's overall strategy by effectively isolating Sickles' corps from the rest of the Union line and exposing the Union left flank in the process. By the early afternoon of July 2, nothing but the fog of war was preventing the Confederates from turning and crushing Sickles' forces, then moving to outflank the entire Union Army.

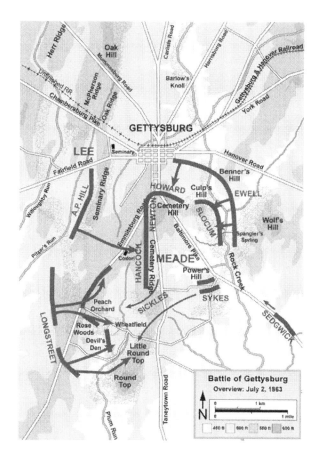

With General George Meade once again in command, General Hancock and the II Corps was positioned on Cemetery Ridge, roughly in the center of the Union line. Since Lee intended to strike at both Union flanks, theoretically Hancock's men should very well not have been engaged at all on the second day of the battle. But as a result of the fact Sickles had moved his men so far out of position, it created a major gap in the Union line and brought the III Corps directly into Longstreet's path. It was 4:00 p.m. by the time Longstreet's two divisions were in position for the attack, and they were taken completely by surprise when they found the III Corps in front of them on the Emmitsburg Road. Hood lobbied Longstreet to change up the plan of attack, seeing the same problems Longstreet had presented to Lee, but at this late time in the day Longstreet refused to modify Lee's orders.

Thus, in the late afternoon, the fighting on Day 2 began in earnest, and Longstreet's assault commenced by smashing into Sickles III Corps, engaging them in a peach orchard, wheat field, and Devil's Den, an outcropping of boulders that provided the Confederates prime cover.

At the same time, men from Confederate General A. P. Hill's corps made their advance toward the Union center, forcing the Army of the Potomac to rally defenses and rushed unit to critical spots to patch the holes. With Hill in his front and Longstreet's attack to his left, Hancock was in the unenviable position of having to attempt to resist Confederate advances spread out over a few miles, at least until more and more reserves could be rushed over from the other side of the Union line to the army's left flank. At one point, Hancock ordered a regiment to make what was essentially a suicidal bayonet charge into the face of Hill's Confederates on Cemetery Ridge. Hancock sent the First Minnesota to charge a Confederate brigade four times its size. One of the Minnesota volunteers, one William Lochren later said, "Every man realized in an instant what the order meant -- death or wounds to us all; the sacrifice of the regiment to gain a few minutes time and save the position, and probably the battlefield -- and every man saw and accepted the necessity of the sacrifice."[13] While extremely costly to the regiment (the Minnesotans suffered 87% casualties, the worst of any regiment at Gettysburg), this heroic sacrifice bought time to organize the defensive line and kept the battle from turning in favor of the Confederates. Hancock would write of them, "I cannot speak too highly of this regiment and its commander in its attack, as well as in its subsequent advance against the enemy, in which it lost three-fourths of the officers and men engaged."

As Longstreet's assault on the Union left continued, his line naturally got more and more entangled as well. As Longstreet's men kept moving to their right, they reached the base of Little Round Top and Round Top, two rocky hills south of Gettysburg proper, at the far left. When Meade's chief engineer, Brig. General Gouverneur Warren, spotted the sun shining off the bayonets of Longstreet's men as they moved toward the Union left, it alerted the Army of the Potomac of the need to occupy Little Round Top, high ground that commanded much of the field.

With Warren having alerted his superiors to the importance of Little Round Top, Strong Vincent's brigade moved into position, under orders from Warren to "hold this ground at any costs," As part of Strong Vincent's brigade, Chamberlain's 20th Maine was on the left of the line, and thus Chamberlain's unit represented the extreme left of the Army of the Potomac's line.

In front of Vincent's brigade was General Evander Law's advancing Alabama Brigade (of Hood's Division). Law ordered 5 regiments to take Little Round Top, the 4th, 15th, and 47th

13   Davis, Kenneth C. *The Civil War: Everything You Need to Know About America's Greatest Conflict but Never Learned*. Page 301.

Alabama, and the 4th and 5th Texas, but they had already marched more than 20 miles just to reach that point. They were now being asked to charge up high ground on a muggy, hot day.

Nevertheless, the Confederates made desperate assaults against Little Round Top, even after being repulsed by the Union defenders several times. In the middle of the fighting, after he saw Confederates trying to push around his flank, Chamberlain stretched his line until his regiment was merely a single-file line, and he then had to order his left (southernmost) half to swing back, thus forming an angle in their line in an effort to prevent a flank attack. Despite suffering heavy losses, the 20th Maine held through two subsequent charges by the 15th Alabama and other Confederate regiments for nearly 2 hours.

Chamberlain

Even after repulsing the Confederates several times, Chamberlain and his regiment faced a serious dilemma. With casualties mounting and ammunition running low, in desperation, Chamberlain *claimed* to have ordered his left wing to initiate an all-out, pivoting bayonet charge. With the 20th Maine charging ahead, the left wing wheeling continually to make the charging line swing like a hinge, thus creating a simultaneous frontal assault and flanking maneuver, they ultimately succeeded in not only taking the hill, but capturing 100 Confederate soldiers in the process. Chamberlain suffered two slight wounds in the battle, one when a shot ricocheted off his sword scabbard and bruised his thigh, another when his right foot was struck by a piece of shrapnel. With this success, Chamberlain was credited with preventing the Union flank from being penetrated and keeping the Confederates from pouring in behind Union lines.

Ultimately, it was the occupation and defense of Little Round Top that saved the rest of the Union line at Gettysburg. Had the Confederates commanded that high ground, it would have been able to position artillery that could have swept the Union lines along Cemetery Ridge and

Cemetery Hill, which would have certainly forced the Army of the Potomac to withdraw from their lines. Chamberlain would be awarded the coveted Congressional Medal of Honor for "daring heroism and great tenacity in holding his position on the Little Round Top against repeated assaults, and carrying the advance position on the Great Round Top", and the 20th Maine's actions that day became one of the most famous attacks of the Battle of Gettysburg and the Civil War as a whole.

But did it really happen that way? Though historians have mostly given Chamberlain the credit for the order to affix bayonets and make the charge down Little Round Top, and Chamberlain received the credit from Sharaa's *The Killer Angels* and the movie *Gettysburg*, some recent researchers have claimed that Lt. Holman S. Melcher initiated the charge. According to Chamberlain however, Melcher had requested permission to make an advance to help some of his wounded men, only to be told by Chamberlain that a charge was about to be ordered anyway.

While Chamberlain's men held the extreme left, the rest of Vincent's brigade struggled desperately to the right, and Vincent himself would be mortally wounded in the fighting. The Confederates had advanced as far as Devil's Den, but Warren continued to bring reinforcements to Little Round Top to hold off Confederate attempts on the high ground. For the rest of the battle, even after the Confederates were repulsed from Little Round Top, their snipers in Devil's Den made the defenders of Little Round Top miserable. Confederate sharpshooters stationed around Devil's Den mortally wounded General Stephen Weed, whose New York brigade had arrived as reinforcements, and when his friend, artilleryman Lt. Charles Hazlett leaned over to comfort Weed or hear what he was trying to say, snipers shot Hazlett dead as well.

The fighting on the Union left finally ended as night fell. George Sykes, the commander of the V Corps, later described Day 2 in his official report, "Night closed the fight. The key of the battle-field was in our possession intact. Vincent, Weed, and Hazlett, chiefs lamented throughout the corps and army, sealed with their lives the spot intrusted to their keeping, and on which so much depended.... General Weed and Colonel Vincent, officers of rare promise, gave their lives to their country."

Ewell's orders from Lee had been to launch a demonstration on the Union right flank during Longstreet's attack, which started at about 4:00 p.m. as well, and in support of the demonstration by Hill's corps in the center. For that reason, Ewell would not launch his general assault on Culp's Hill and Cemetery Hill until 7:00 p.m.

While the Army of the Potomac managed to desperately hold on the left, Ewell's attack against Culp's Hill on the other end of the field met with some success in pushing the Army of the Potomac back. However, the attack started so late in the day that nightfall made it impossible for the Confederates to capitalize on their success. Due to darkness, a Confederate brigade led by

George H. Steuart was unaware that they were firmly beside the Army of the Potomac's right flank, which would have given them almost unlimited access to the Union army's rear and its supply lines and line of communication, just 600 yards away. the main line of communication for the Union army, the Baltimore Pike, only 600 yards to their front. Col. David Ireland and the 137th New York desperately fought to preserve the Union army's flank, much the same way Chamberlain and the 20th Maine had on the other side, and in the process the 137th lost a third of their men.

Ewell's men would spend the night at the base of Culp's Hill and partially up the hill, in positions that had been evacuated by Union soldiers after Meade moved some of them to the left to deal with Longstreet's attack. It would fall upon the Confederates to pick up the attack the next morning.

Though having gotten a late start, Pickett and his men made haste, arriving exhausted, about three miles east of Gettysburg late in the afternoon of July 2. Upon arrival, Pickett discovered that though Lee's Army of Northern Virginia had initially driven the Union Army of the Potomac to the high ground south of Gettysburg, after two days of heavy fighting, they had been unable to completely dislodge the Union soldiers from their position. Pickett reported to Lee that his men would be ready to join the fighting that evening if given a couple hours' rest, but Lee sent word for Pickett to bivouac his men on the Chambersburg Pike until morning (July 3); they wouldn't be used that day.

That night, Meade held another council of war. Having been attacked on both flanks, Meade and his top officers correctly surmised that Lee would attempt an attack on the center of the line the next day. Moreover, captured Confederates and the fighting and intelligence of Day 2 let it be known that the only Confederate unit that had not yet seen action during the fighting was Pickett's division of Longstreet's corps.

Chapter 12: July 3, 1863

Lee's Plans

If July 2 was Longstreet's worst day of the Civil War, July 3 was almost certainly Robert E. Lee's. After the attack on July 2, Longstreet spent the night continuing to plot potential movements around Little Round Top and Big Round Top, thinking that would again get the Confederate army around the Union's flank. Longstreet himself did not realize that a reserve corps of the Union army was poised to block that maneuver.

Longstreet did not meet with Lee on the night of July 2, so when Lee met with him the following morning he found Longstreet's men were not ready to conduct an early morning attack, which Lee had wanted to attempt just as he was on the other side of the lines against

Culp's Hill. With Pickett's men not up, however, Longstreet's corps couldn't make such an attack. Lee later wrote that Longstreet's "dispositions were not completed as early as was expected."

When Lee learned Longstreet couldn't commence an attack in the early morning, he attempted to stop Ewell from launching one, but by then it was too late. Ewell's men engaged in fighting along Culp's Hill, until the fighting fizzled out around noon. By then, Lee had already planned a massive attack on the Union center, combined with having Stuart's cavalry attack the Union army's lines in the rear. A successful attack would split the Army of the Potomac at the same time its communication and supply lines were severed by Stuart, which would make it possible to capture the entire army in detail.

There was just one problem with the plan, as Longstreet told Lee that morning: no 15,000 men who ever existed could successfully execute the attack. The charge required marching across an open field for about a mile, with the Union artillery holding high ground on all sides of the incoming Confederates. Longstreet ardently opposed the attack, but, already two days into the battle, Lee explained that because the Army of the Potomac was here on the field, he must strike at it. Longstreet later wrote that he said, "General, I have been a soldier all my life. I have been with soldiers engaged in fights by couples, by squads, companies, regiments, divisions, and armies, and should know, as well as any one, what soldiers can do. It is my opinion that no fifteen thousand men ever arrayed for battle can take that position."[14] Longstreet proposed instead that their men should slip around the Union forces and occupy the high ground, forcing Northern commanders to attack them, rather than *vice versa*.

Realizing the insanity of sending 15,000 men hurtling into all the Union artillery, Lee planned to use the Confederate artillery to try to knock out the Union artillery ahead of time. Although old friend William Pendleton was the artillery chief, the artillery cannonade would be supervised by Edward Porter Alexander, Longstreet's chief artillerist, who would have to give the go-ahead to the charging infantry because they were falling under Longstreet's command. Alexander later noted that Longstreet was so disturbed and dejected about ordering the attack that at one point he tried to make Alexander order the infantry forward, essentially doing Longstreet's dirty work for him.

---

[14]   Gaffney, P. and D. Gaffney. *The Civil War: Exploring History One Week at a Time*. Page 282.

Alexander

As Longstreet had predicted, from the beginning the plan was an abject failure. As Stuart's cavalry met its Union counterparts near East Cavalry Field, a young cavalry officer named George Custer convinced division commander Brig. General David McMurtrie Gregg to allow his brigade to stay and fight, even while Custer's own division was stationed to the south out of the action.

The fighting at East Cavalry Field turned out to be Custer's best known action of the Civil War, and it was his brigade that bore the brunt of the casualties in repulsing Stuart's cavalry. Right as the Confederates were starting the artillery bombardment ahead of Pickett's Charge,

Stuart's men met Gregg's on the field.

After Stuart's men sent Union skirmishers scurrying, Gregg ordered Custer to counterattack with the 7th Michigan Cavalry Regiment. Custer led the charge personally, exhorting his men with the rallying cry, "Come on you Wolverines!" In the ensuing melee, which featured sabers and close range shooting, Custer had his horse shot out from under him, at which point he took a bugler's horse and continued fighting. Ultimately, his men sent Stuart's cavalry retreating, forcing Stuart to order in reinforcements.

Stuart's reinforcements sent the 7th Michigan in retreat, but now Custer rallied the 1st Michigan regiment to charge in yet another counterattack, with the same rallying cry, ""Come on you Wolverines!" Both sides galloped toward each other and crashed head on, engaging in more fierce hand-to-hand combat. Eventually, the Union held the field and forced Stuart's men to retreat.

Custer's brigade lost over 200 men in the attack, the highest loss of any Union cavalry brigade at Gettysburg, but he had just valiantly performed one of the most successful cavalry charges of the war. Custer wasn't exactly humble about his performance, writing in his official report after the battle, "I challenge the annals of warfare to produce a more brilliant or successful charge of cavalry."

Pickett's Charge

Longstreet was certain of failure, but Pickett and the men preparing to make the charge were confident in their commanders and themselves. As Stuart was in the process of being repulsed, just after 1:00 p.m. 150 Confederate guns began to fire from Seminary Ridge, hoping to incapacitate the Union center before launching an infantry attack. Confederate brigadier Evander Law said of the artillery bombardment, "The cannonade in the center ... presented one of the most magnificent battle-scenes witnessed during the war. Looking up the valley towards Gettysburg, the hills on either side were capped with crowns of flame and smoke, as 300 guns, about equally divided between the two ridges, vomited their iron hail upon each other."

Meanwhile, at daylight Pickett had advanced his division to a spot "into a field near a branch," a few hundred yards behind the main Confederate line on Seminary Ridge. Forming battlelines, his men advanced east a few hundred yards before being ordered to lie down and wait. Advancing again through Spangler's Woods, they were again directed to lay down—this time behind the crest on which the Confederate artillery batteries were perched. Jocking for position to form the right wing of the afternoon's assault, Pickett then had his men form two lines, with Brigadier Generals James Kemper and Richard Garnett in the first line, right to left, and Brigadier General Lewis Armistead to the rear. As a result, Pickett's men were forced to lay down during a ferocious artillery bombardment from both sides that certainly had to unnerve his men, but Pickett continued a dangerous ride along the lines as Union shells burst all around him, shouting to his men, "Up, men, and to your posts! Don't forget today that you are from Old Virginia."[15]

Unfortunately for the Confederates, their artillery mostly overshot their mark. The artillery duel could be heard from dozens of miles away, and all the smoke led to Confederate artillery constantly overshooting their targets. Realizing that the Confederate artillery was meant for them as a way of softening them up for an infantry charge, Hancock calmly rode his horse up and down the line of the II Corps, both inspiring and assuring his men with his own courage and resolve. During the massive Confederate artillery bombardment that preceded the infantry assault, Hancock was so conspicuous on horseback reviewing and encouraging his troops that one of his subordinates pleaded with him that "the corps commander ought not to risk his life that way." Hancock reportedly replied, "There are times when a corps commander's life does not count."

Eventually, Union artillery chief Henry Hunt cleverly figured that if the Union cannons stopped firing back, the Confederates might think they successfully knocked out the Union batteries. On top of that, the Union would be preserving its ammunition for the impending charge that everyone now knew was coming. When they stopped, Lee, Alexander, and others mistakenly concluded that they'd knocked out the Union artillery.

At some point before the charge, Pickett apparently managed to hastily write a letter to Sallie:

"At early dawn, darkened by the threatening rain, Armistead, Garnett, Kemper and your Soldier held a heart-to-heart powwow.

All three sent regards to you, and Old Lewis pulled a ring from his little finger and making me take it, said, "Give this little token, George, please, to her of the sunset eyes, with my love, and tell her the 'old man' says since he could not be the lucky dog he's mighty glad that you are."

Dear old Lewis—dear old "Lo," as Magruder always called him, being short for Lothario. Well, my Sally, I'll keep the ring for you, and some day I'll take it to John Tyler and have it made into a breastpin and set around with rubies and diamonds and emeralds. You will be the pearl, the other jewel. Dear old Lewis!

Just as we three separated to go our different ways after silently clasping hands, our fears and prayers voiced in the "Good luck, old man," a summons came from Old Peter, and I immediately rode to the top of the ridge where he and Marse Robert were making a reconnaissance of Meade's position. "Great God!" said Old Peter as I came up. "Look,

[15] Vectorsite.net, "July 1863 (3): Don't Forget Today That You Are From Old Virginia."

General Lee, at the insurmountable difficulties between our line and that of the Yankees—the steep hills, the tiers of artillery, the fences, the heavy skirmish line—and then we'll have to fight our infantry against their batteries. Look at the ground we'll have to charge over, nearly a mile of that open ground there under the rain of their canister and shrapnel."

"The enemy is there, General Longstreet, and I am going to strike him," said Marse Robert in his firm, quiet, determined voice.

About 8 o'clock I rode with them along our line of prostrate infantry. They had been told to lie down to prevent attracting attention, and though they had been forbidden to cheer they voluntarily arose and lifted in reverential adoration their caps to our beloved commander as we rode slowly along. Oh, the responsibility for the lives of such men as these! Well, my darling, their fate and that of our beloved Southland will be settled ere your glorious brown eyes rest on these scraps of penciled paper—your Soldier's last letter, perhaps.

Our line of battle faces Cemetery Ridge. Our detachments have been thrown forward to support our artillery which stretches over a mile along the crests of Oak Ridge and Seminary Ridge. The men are lying in the rear, my darling, and the hot July sun pours its scorching rays almost vertically down upon them. The suffering and waiting are almost unbearable.

. . . .

Well, my sweetheart, at one o'clock the awful silence was broken by a cannon-shot and then another, and then more than a hundred guns shook the hills from crest to base, answered by more than another hundred—the whole world a blazing volcano, the whole of heaven a thunderbolt—then darkness and absolute silence—then the grim and gruesome, low-spoken commands—then the forming of the attacking columns. My brave Virginians are to attack in front. Oh, may God in mercy help me as He never helped before!

I have ridden up to report to Old Peter. I shall give him this letter to mail to you and a package to give you if—Oh, my darling, do you feel the love of my heart, the prayer, as I write that fatal word?

Now, I go; but remember always that I love you with all my heart and soul, with every fiber of my being; that now and forever I am yours—yours, my beloved. It is almost three o'clock. My soul reaches out to yours—my prayers. I'll keep up a skookum tumtum for Virginia and for you, my darling."

A short time later, the Confederates were prepared to step out for the charge that bears Pickett's name, even though he commanded only about a third of the force and was officially under Longstreet's direction. Today historians typically refer to the charge as the Pickett-Pettigrew-Trimble Assault or Longstreet's Assault to be more technically correct. Since A.P. Hill was sidelined with illness, Pettigrew's and Trimble's divisions were delegated to Longstreet's authority as well. To make matters worse, Hill's sickness resulted in organizational snafus. Without Hill to assign or lead troops, some of his battle-weary soldiers of the previous two days were tapped to make the charge while fresh soldiers in his corps stayed behind.

Just before 2:00 p.m. (while said to be writing a farewell letter to Sallie, a courier brought a note to Pickett from artillery commander Porter Alexander warning him that unless he moved his men quickly they would not have sufficient artillery cover because ammunition was already running low. .The charge was to begin with Pickett's division of Virginians, and shortly after the Union guns fell silent, with his men in position, Pickett showed the note to his commander and asked Longstreet to give the order to advance. Longstreet could only nod, fearing that "to verbalize the order may reveal his utter lack of confidence in the plan." With that, around 2:00 p.m. about 12,500-15,000 Confederates stepped out in sight and began their charge with an orderly march starting about a mile away, no doubt an inspiring sight to the Union men directly across from the oncoming assault.

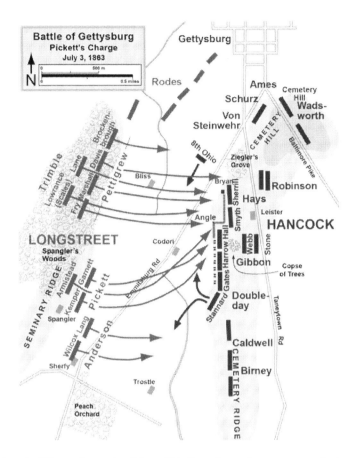

Pickett launched his attack as ordered, but within five minutes the men came to the top of a low rise where his line came into full view of Union defenses. Though Pickett was seen galloping to the left to steady his men there, and one aide is said to remember him personally ordering the division to "double-quick" at the end of the advance, his exact whereabouts during the latter stages of the assault are unknown.

As the Confederate line advanced, Union cannon on Cemetery Ridge and Little Round Top began blasting away, with Confederate soldiers continuing to march forward. One Union soldier later wrote, "We could not help hitting them with every shot . . . a dozen men might be felled by one single bursting shell."[16] By the time Longstreet's men reached Emmitsburg Road, Union artillery switched to firing grapeshot (tin cans filled with iron and lead balls), and as the Confederate troops continued to approach the Union center, Union troops positioned behind the wall cut down the oncoming Confederates, easily decimating both flanks. Lt. Col. Franklin Sawyer of the 8th Ohio reported, "They were at once enveloped in a dense cloud of smoke and dust. Arms, heads, blankets, guns and knapsacks were thrown and tossed in to the clear air. ... A moan went up from the field, distinctly to be heard amid the storm of battle."

After about 20 minutes, the Confederates had managed to cross the shallow valley but then hit the stone fence shielding Union soldiers (in some places, two-men deep). And although Pickett's men were finally able to reach and breach the Union line on the ridge, what followed next has been categorically described as a "blood bath." While some of the men did manage to advance to the Union line and engage in hand-to-hand combat, it was of little consequence. In the midst of the fighting, as he was conferring with one of his brigadier generals, General Stannard, Hancock suddenly felt a searing pain in his thigh. He had just been severely wounded when a bullet struck the pommel of his saddle and entered his inner right thigh, along with wood splinters and a large bent nail. Helped from his horse by his aides, he removed the saddle nail himself and applied a tourniquet, colorfully swearing at his own men while demanding that they not let him bleed to death. Nevertheless, he refused to remove himself to the rear until the offensive had concluded.

According to Longstreet, it was Pickett who finally called retreat; after about an hour, nearly 6,500 Confederates were dead or wounded, five times that of the Union, with all 13 regimental commanders in Pickett's division killed or wounded. One of the Virginians who marched straight into Hancock's II Corps was Pickett's brigadier Lewis A. Armistead, who famously led his brigade with his hat atop his sword, serving as a visual cue for his men. They actually breached the II Corps' line, making it about as far as any Confederate got. In the fighting, Armistead was mortally wounded and captured, dying days later.

Trimble and Pettigrew, the other two leaders of the charge, were both wounded in the fighting, with Trimble losing a leg and Pettigrew suffering a minor wound to the hand. In addition to Armistead's mortal wounding, Kemper was seriously wounded and captured. Meanwhile Richard Garnett, whose courage had been impugned and challenged by Stonewall Jackson unfairly in 1862, had suffered a previous leg injury and insisted on riding his horse during the charge, despite the obvious fact that riding a horse clearly indicated he was an officer. Garnett was killed during the charge, and it's unknown where he fell or where he was buried.

In the aftermath of the defeat, General Longstreet stated, "General Lee came up as our troops were falling back and encouraged them as well as he could; begged them to reform their ranks and reorganize their forces . . . and it was then he used the expression . . . 'It was all my fault; get

---

[16]   Gaffney, P. and D. Gaffney. *The Civil War: Exploring History One Week at a Time*. Page 283.

together, and let us do the best we can toward saving which is left to us.'"[17]

Today Pickett's Charge is remembered as the American version of the Charge of the Light Brigade, a heroic but completely futile march that had no chance of success. In fact, it's remembered as Pickett's Charge because Pickett's Virginians wanted to claim the glory of getting the furthest during the attack in the years after the war.

The charge suffered about a 50% casualty rate, as the Confederates marched into hell. The men barely made a dent in the Union line before retreating in disorder back across the field, where Lee met them in an effort to regroup them in case the Union counterattacked. At one point, Lee ordered Pickett to reform his division, to which Pickett reportedly cried, "I have no division!" Pickett's post-battle report was apparently so bitter that Lee ordered it destroyed. Though the charge was named Pickett's Charge by newspapers for the purpose of praising Pickett's Virginians for making the furthest progress, Pickett felt the charge had tarnished his career, and he remained upset that his name remained associated with the sharply repulsed attack. Furthermore, Pickett himself has received much criticism (both then and to this day) for surviving the battle unscathed, having established his final position well to the rear of his troops, though any charges of cowardice are strongly contradicted by his record earlier in the war and in Mexico.

After the battle, Pickett wrote to Sallie offering a few details about the fateful charge. Since his official report of the battle has never been found, possibly a result of Lee having ordered him to rewrite if because his original was too negative, his letters home were his only words about the events:

"MY letter of yesterday, my darling, written before the battle, was full of hope and cheer; even though it told you of the long hours of waiting from four in the morning, when Gary's pistol rang out from the Federal lines signaling the attack upon Culp's Hill, to the solemn eight-o'clock review of my men, who rose and stood silently lifting their hats in loving reverence as Marse Robert, Old Peter and your own Soldier reviewed them—on then to the deadly stillness of the five hours following, when the men lay in the tall grass in the rear of the artillery line, the July sun pouring its scorching rays almost vertically down upon them, till one o'clock when the awful silence of the vast battlefield was broken by a cannon-shot which opened the greatest artillery duel of the world. The firing lasted two hours. When it ceased we took advantage of the blackened field and in the glowering darkness formed our attacking column just before the brow of Seminary Ridge.

[17]   Davis, Kenneth C. *The Civil War: Everything You Need to Know About America's Greatest Conflict but Never Learned.* Page 306.

I closed my letter to you a little before three o'clock and rode up to Old Peter for orders. I found him like a great lion at bay. I have never seen him so grave and troubled. For several minutes after I had saluted him he looked at me without speaking. Then in an agonized voice, the reserve all gone, he said:

"Pickett, I am being crucified at the thought of the sacrifice of life which this attack will make. I have instructed Alexander to watch the effect of our fire upon the enemy, and when it begins to tell he must take the responsibility and give you your orders, for I can't."

While he was yet speaking a note was brought to me from Alexander. After reading it I handed it to him, asking if I should obey and go forward. He looked at me for a moment, then held out his hand. Presently, clasping his other hand over mine without speaking he bowed his head upon his breast. I shall never forget the look in his face nor the clasp of his hand when I said:—"Then, General, I shall lead my Division on." I had ridden only a few paces when I remembered your letter and (forgive me) thoughtlessly scribbled in a corner of the envelope, "If Old Peter's nod means death then good-by and God bless you, little one," turned back and asked the dear old chief if he would be good enough to mail it for me. As he took your letter from me, my darling, I saw tears glistening on his cheeks and beard. The stern old war-horse, God bless him, was weeping for his men and, I know, praying too that this cup might pass from them. I obeyed the silent assent of his bowed head, an assent given against his own convictions,—given in anguish and with reluctance.

My brave boys were full of hope and confident of victory as I led them forth, forming them in column of attack, and though officers and men alike knew what was before them,—knew the odds against them,—they eagerly offered up their lives on the altar of duty, having absolute faith in their ultimate success. Over on Cemetery Ridge the Federals beheld a scene never before witnessed on this continent,—a scene which has never previously been enacted and can never take place again—an army forming in line of battle in full view, under their very eyes—charging across a space nearly a mile in length over fields of waving grain and anon of stubble and then a smooth expanse— moving with the steadiness of a dress parade, the pride and glory soon to be crushed by an overwhelming heartbreak.

. . . .

Well, it is all over now. The battle is lost, and many of us are prisoners, many are dead, many wounded, bleeding and dying. Your Soldier lives and mourns and but for you, my darling, he would rather, a million times rather, be back there with his dead, to sleep for all time in an unknown grave."

Days later, Pickett wrote yet another tense letter back to Sallie, in which his angst can be felt:

General Lee's letter has been published to the division in general orders and received with appreciative satisfaction. The soldiers, one and all, love and honor Lee, and his sympathy and praise are always very dear to them. Just after the order was published I heard one of the men, rather rough and uncouth and not, as are most of the men, to the manner born, say, as he wiped away the tears with the back of his hand, "Dag-gone him, dag-gone him, dag-gone his old soul, I'm blamed ef I wouldn't be dag-gone willin' to go right through it all and be killed again with them others to hear Marse Robert, dag-gone him, say over again as how he grieved bout'n we-all's losses and honored us for we-all's bravery! Darned ef I wouldn't." Isn't that reverential adoration, my darling, to be willing to be "killed again" for a word of praise?

It seems selfish and inhuman to speak of Love—haunted as I am with the unnecessary sacrifice of the lives of so many of my brave boys. I can't think of anything but the desolate homes in Virginia and the unknown dead in Pennsylvania. At the beginning of the fight I was so sanguine, so sure of success! Early in the morning I had been assured by Alexander that General Lee had ordered that every brigade in his command was to charge Cemetery Hill; so I had no fear of not being supported. Alexander also assured me of the support of his artillery which would move ahead of my division in the advance. He told me that he had borrowed seven twelve-pound howitzers from Pendleton, Lee's Chief of Artillery, which he had put in reserve to accompany me.

In the morning I rode with him while he, by Longstreet's orders, selected the salient angle of the wood in which my line was formed, which line was just on the left of his seventy-five guns. At about a quarter to three o'clock, when his written order to make the charge was handed to me, and dear Old Peter after reading it in sorrow and fear reluctantly bowed his head in assent, I obeyed, leading my three brigades straight on the enemy's front. You never saw anything like it. They moved across that field of death as a battalion marches forward in line of battle upon drill, each commander in front of his command leading and cheering on his men. Two lines of the enemy's infantry were driven back; two lines of guns were taken—and no support came. Pendleton, without Alexander's knowledge, had sent four of the guns which he had loaned him to some other part of the field, and the other three guns could not be found. The two brigades which were to have followed me had, poor fellows, been seriously engaged in the fights of the two previous days. Both of their commanding officers had been killed, and while they had been replaced by gallant, competent officers, these new leaders were unknown to the men.

Ah, if I had only had my other two brigades a different story would have been flashed to the world. It was too late to retreat, and to go on was death or capture. Poor old Dick Garnett did not dismount, as did the others of us, and he was killed instantly, falling from his horse. Kemper, desperately wounded, was brought from the field and subsequently, taken prisoner. Dear old Lewis Armistead, God bless him, was mortally wounded at the head of his command after planting the flag of Virginia within the enemy's lines. Seven of my colonels were killed, and one was mortally wounded. Nine of my lieutenant colonels were wounded, and three lieutenant colonels were killed. Only one field officer of my whole command, Colonel Cabell, was unhurt, and the loss of my company officers was in proportion.

I wonder, my dear, if in the light of the Great Eternity we shall any of us feel this was for the best and shall have learned to say, "Thy will be done."

No castles to-day, sweetheart. No, the bricks of happiness and the mortar of love must lie untouched in this lowering gloom. Pray, dear, for the sorrowing ones."

Chapter 13: Who's to Blame?

Lee?

From almost the moment the Civil War ended, Gettysburg has been widely viewed as one of the decisive turning points of the Civil War. As renowned Civil War historian described Gettysburg, "It might be less of a victory than Mr. Lincoln had hoped for, but it was nevertheless a victory—and, because of that, it was no longer possible for the Confederacy to win the war. The North might still lose it, to be sure, if the soldiers or the people should lose heart, but outright defeat was no longer in the cards." While some still dispute that labeling, Lee's Army of Northern Virginia was never truly able to take the strategic offensive again for the duration of the war.

Naturally, if Gettysburg marked an important turning point in the Civil War, then to the defeated South it represented one of the last true opportunities the South had to win the war. After the South had lost the war, the importance of Gettysburg as one of the "high tide" marks of the Confederacy became apparent to everyone, making the battle all the more important in the years after it had been fought. Former Confederate comrades like Longstreet and Jubal Early would go on to argue who was responsible for the loss at Gettysburg (and thus the war) in the following decades. Much of the debate was fueled by those who wanted to protect Lee's legacy, especially because Lee was dead and could not defend himself in writing anymore. However, on July 3, Lee insisted on taking full blame for what occurred at Gettysburg, telling his retreating men, "It's all my fault." Historians have mostly agreed, placing the blame for the disastrous Day 3 on Lee's shoulders. Porter Alexander would later call it Lee's "worst day" of the war.

Ironically, though he had no use for post-war politics, Lee's legacy was crafted and embroiled in it. Though Lee accepted the South's loss, unreconstructed rebels continued to "fight" the Civil War with the pen, aiming to influence how the war was remembered. Much of this was accomplished by the Southern Historical Society, whose stated aim was the homogenization of Southern white males. But longstanding feuds between former generals found their way into the papers, and the feuds were frequently based on regional differences. These former Confederates looked to their idealized war heroes as symbols of their suffering and struggle. Based in Richmond, the Society's ideal Southern white male embodied the "Virginian" essence of aristocracy, morality and chivalry. The Society's ideal male, of course, was Robert E. Lee. David Blight credits the Society for creating a "Lee cult" that dominates public perception to this day. Writing about this perception of Lee, Charles Osbourne described the perception as "an edifice of myth built on the foundation of truth…the image became an icon."

Still, Lee was far from perfect, despite the attempts of the Southern Historical Society to defend his war record as fault free, at the expense of some of his subordinates. Given that the Confederacy lost the war, some historians have pointed out that Lee was often too eager to engage in offensive warfare. After all, Lee scored large and smashing victories at places like Chancellorsville that deprived him of more manpower against opponents that could afford casualties more than he could. Moreover, for the engineer who used tactics to successfully defend against typical Civil War tactics, he all too often engaged in the same futile offensive tactics himself, none more costly than Pickett's Charge.

Longstreet?

However, after the war, former Confederates would not accept criticism of Lee, and blame for the loss at Gettysburg was thus placed upon other scapegoats. Although it was not immediately apparent where the blame rested for such a devastating loss, not long after the Battle of Gettysburg two names kept surfacing: cavalry leader General "Jeb" Stuart and General James Longstreet; Stuart blamed for robbing Lee of the "eyes" he needed to know of Union movement, and Longstreet for delaying his attack on Round Top Hills the second day and acting too slowly in executing the assault on the Union left flank.

Long before Gettysburg, Longstreet was characterized by his men and commanders as "congenitally resistant to hurry himself,"[18] resistant to change of orders (even from his supreme commander, Lee), and disliked to overextend his men (once bivouacked, he allowed his men to

---

[18]   Dowdey, Clifford. *Lee's Last Campaign: The Story of Lee & His Men against Grant--1864.* Page 134.

prepare three-days' rations before breaking camp, even when they were supposed to stick to a timetable). In fact, his designation as Lee's "old reliable" appears to have been bestowed by someone who had never actually worked with him or had to rely upon him.

Similarly, Longstreet's clash with A. P. Hill, then Jackson, Hood and Toombs, were indicative of his unwillingness to accept that he was not the center of attention; not the one destined for greatness. And, of course, as the War progressed, Longstreet's propensity to find fault (and start feuds) with Lafayette McLaws (who he tried to have court-martialed), Evander Law (who he tried to have arrested), Charles Field, and ultimately, Lee himself, was highly indicative of the self-possessed illusion Longstreet was living (and fighting) under. While always quick to reprimand any subordinate who questioned his orders, he clearly hesitated to resist orders from his superiors on occasions. In his Gettysburg account, Longstreet had the impudence to blame Lee for "not changing his plans" based on Longstreet's "want of confidence in them."

After General Robert E. Lee died in October of 1870, a group of ex-Confederates led by General Jubal Early (who had led a division in Ewell's corps at Gettysburg) publicly criticized Longstreet for ignoring orders and delaying his attack on the second day of the Battle on July 2, 1863. But while many former Confederates held Longstreet accountable for not following orders, Early took it one step further, arguing that Longstreet -- not Lee -- was responsible for the Confederate defeat (deemed a "tactical disaster" by most) that by most accounts was the beginning of the end for the Confederacy.

Early

In his memoirs, however, Longstreet defended himself, saying that the blistering post-War attacks concerning Gettysburg were merely "payback for supporting Black suffrage", thus shifting the blame back to Lee. He wrote, "[Lee] knew that I did not believe that success was possible . . . he should have put an officer in charge who had more confidence in his plan."[19] He went on to say that Lee should have given the responsibility to Early, thus justifying his insubordination.

On the other hand, Longstreet's reputation has mostly been on the upswing in the past few decades, due in no small part to Michael Shaara's 1974 novel *The Killer Angels*, which portrayed Longstreet in a more flattering light. That novel was the basis for the 1993 film *Gettysburg*, which has also helped rehabilitate Longstreet's legacy and helped make clear to the public how instrumental he was during the war. In 1982, Thomas L. Connolly and Barbara L. Bellows published *God and General Longstreet*, which took the Lost Cause proponents like Early to task for their blatant fabrications (such as the one that Lee ordered Longstreet to attack in the early morning of Day 2 of Gettysburg), helping make clear the extent of historical revision propagated by the Lost Cause. In doing so, they cast Longstreet as a sympathetic victim of circumstances and sectional and political hostility.

It's also important to note that Lee himself never made any post-War statements to suggest that he held Longstreet responsible for the Confederacy's demise.

Stuart?

Outwardly, Stuart was the embodiment of reckless courage, magnificent manhood, and unconquerable virility; a man who could wear--without drawing suspicion of instability--the flamboyant adornments of a classic cavalier. It was once written that his black plume and hat caught up with a golden star, seemed the proper frame for a knightly face. In that same vein, people were always aware that Stuart was engaging in public relations even then, and Civil War historian Jeff Wert captured it well: "Stuart had been the Confederacy's knight-errant, the bold and dashing cavalier, attired in a resplendent uniform, plumed hat, and cape. Amid a slaughterhouse, he had embodied chivalry, clinging to the pageantry of a long-gone warrior. He crafted the image carefully, and the image befitted him. He saw himself as the Southern people envisaged him. They needed a knight; he needed to be that knight." Stuart, in effect, was the very essence of the Lost Cause.

It has been widely presumed that those same vainglorious traits led Stuart on a glory-seeking mission near the end of June 1863, which badly damaged Lee's abilities in Pennsylvania and directly led to the Army of Northern Virginia stumbling into a general battle Lee wished to avoid. Though credited with devoting his full attention to the Confederate cause upon his arrival, many historians attribute the catastrophic loss to the absence of Stuart and his cavalry.

---

[19]   Gaffney, P., and D. Gaffney. *The Civil War: Exploring History One Week at a Time.* Page 442.

Immediately becoming the most devastating event of Stuart's military career, in his official report General Lee's wrote, " . . . the absence of the cavalry rendered it impossible to obtain accurate information. By the route [we] pursued, the Federal Army was interposed between [my] command and our main body, preventing any communication with [Stuart] until his arrival at Carlisle. The march toward Gettysburg was conducted more slowly than it would have been had the movements of the Federal Army been known." Some of Stuart's subordinates would come to his defense after the war, and Lee deserves some blame for allowing his subordinates so much discretion, which may have worked with Stonewall Jackson but backfired spectacularly with Ewell and Stuart. After the war, Stuart's subordinate, General Thomas L. Rosser stated what many were already convinced of, "On this campaign, [Stuart] undoubtedly, make the fatal blunder which lost us the battle of Gettysburg."[20]

The Army of the Potomac?

To a great extent, the Confederates' search for scapegoats is a product of the fact that they were so used to being successful that a defeat had to be explained by a Southern failure, not a Northern success.

In casting about for Southern deficiencies, it is often overlooked that Meade and his top subordinates fought a remarkably efficient battle. Meade created an extremely sturdy defensive line anchored on high ground, he held the interior lines by having his army spread out over a smaller area, and he used that ability to shuffle troops from the right to the left on July 2. Moreover, Meade was able to rely on his corps commanders, especially Hancock, to properly use their discretion. Before the battle, Lee reportedly said that Meade "would commit no blunders on my front and if I make one ... will make haste to take advantage of it." If he said it, he was definitely right.

Perhaps none other than George Pickett himself put it best. When asked (certainly ad nauseam) why Pickett's Charge had failed, Pickett is said to have tersely replied, "I've always thought the Yankees had something to do with it."

Chapter 14: Scandal in North Carolina

After Gettysburg, Pickett moved what remained of his decimated division to a secure area of southeastern Virginia, where he bolstered his ranks and replenished supplies. While Longstreet's corps headed west to Tennessee and fought at Chickamauga, Pickett's division stayed east. In January 1864, Pickett led his men into North Carolina, intending to capture the city of New Bern after the Confederacy had tried and failed to capture New Burn earlier in the war. Ultimately failing due to poor planning, Pickett became embroiled in what would become the second major

---

20   Wert, Jeffry D. *Cavalryman of the Lost Cause: A Biography of J.E.B. Stuart*. Page 300.

scandal of his military career.

During the early morning hours of February 2, 1864, 53 North Carolinians were captured by Confederate forces under Pickett's command. Except for a few men who were absent from their unit, these soldiers—caught wearing Union uniforms--represented the entire roster of Company F, Second North Carolina Union Volunteer Infantry; most were either natives of the county in which they were captured or from surrounding counties. Charged categorically with desertion, the men were transported to Confederate prisoner-of-war camps in Richmond, Virginia, and Andersonville, Georgia.

Within four months of their capture, most of the men of Company F were dead, falling victim to any number of diseases contracted while in custody, with 22 publicly hanged in Kinston, North Carolina. Witnessing the soldiers' executions were their wives, friends, neighbors, and former comrades of the Confederate Army. The incident ignited a raging controversy between Union and Confederate authorities and an outcry for justice that would last two years--and did much to further darken Pickett's already tarnished reputation.

While the issue of dealing with "traitors" was cut-and-dry for the Confederacy, the Union had its own perspective: the executed men had been Union soldiers, and as such, deserved to be treated as any other prisoners of war once captured. President Abraham Lincoln had already addressed this point in July of 1863 when he ordered retaliation on Southern prisoners in Northern custody when he ordered that "for every soldier of the United States killed in violation of the laws of war, a rebel soldier shall be executed."[21] News of the Kinston hangings (and the general inhumane treatment Union soldiers were forced to endure in Confederate prisoner-of-war camps) was met with public outrage and demand for revenge—against Pickett.

While the Confederates argued that the 53 North Carolinians were "deserters" who simply received what had long been deemed appropriate punishment for such a crime, in reality the capture and execution was indicative of a much larger issue for the South. From the early days of the War, Confederate field officers had lamented that desertion among Confederate forces was so rampant that while the South was victorious on many battlefields, successes were diluted by the inability to follow-up with further invasion of enemy territory due to lack of manpower. Following his defeat at Antietam, General Robert E. Lee had himself complained to Confederate President Jefferson Davis that a large number of his troops never crossed into Maryland and that "desertion and straggling deprived him of one-third of his effective force," later writing that he feared "nothing but the death penalty, uniformly, inexorably administered, will stop it."[22]

---

[21] Collins, Donald E. *War Crime or Justice? General George Pickett and the Mass Execution of Deserters in Civil War Kinston, North Carolina.*

[22] Collins, Donald E. *War Crime or Justice? General George Pickett and the Mass Execution of*

As Union general Ulysses S. Grant was preparing to launch his Virginia offensive in the spring of 1864, the aftershock of Pickett's North Carolina Campaign spawned great debate and concern regarding the question of how a field general (on either side of the conflict) was to maintain his command in the face of constant desertion. Where does military discipline end and inhumane war atrocity begin? But in that the North had more men at their disposal than did the South, many recognized that one answer might not apply equally in the field; the nation was, after all, at civil "war." Ultimately, Pickett's application of Lee's *suggested* remedy for desertion brought him condemnation as a war criminal himself—charges Pickett would face even after the War.

Chapter 15: The Overland Campaign

With Lee continuing to hold off the Army of the Potomac in a stalemate along the same battle lines at the end of 1863, Lincoln shook things up. In March 1864, Grant was promoted to lieutenant general and given command of all the armies of the United States. His first acts of command were to keep General Halleck in position to serve as a liaison between Lincoln and Secretary of War Edwin Stanton. And though it's mostly forgotten today, Grant technically kept General Meade in command of the Army of the Potomac, even though Grant attached himself to that army before the Overland Campaign in 1864 and thus served as its commander for all intents and purposes.

In May 1864, with Grant now attached to the Army of the Potomac, the Civil War's two most famous generals met each other on the battlefield for the first time. Lee had won stunning victories at battles like Chancellorsville and Second Bull Run by going on the offensive and taking the strategic initiative, but Grant and Lincoln had no intention of letting him do so anymore. Grant ordered General Meade, "Lee's army is your objective point. Wherever Lee goes, there you will go also."

By 1864, things were looking so bleak for the South that the Confederate war strategy was simply to ensure Lincoln lost reelection that November, with the hope that a new Democratic president would end the war and recognize the South's independence. With that, and given the shortage in manpower, Lee's strategic objective was to continue defending Richmond, while hoping that Grant would commit some blunder that would allow him a chance to seize an opportunity.

On May 4, 1864, Grant launched the Overland Campaign, crossing the Rapidan River near Fredericksburg with the 100,000 strong Army of the Potomac, which almost doubled Lee's hardened but battered Army of Northern Virginia. It was a similar position to the one George McClellan had in 1862 and Joe Hooker had in 1863, and Grant's first attack, at the Battle of the

Deserters in Civil War Kinston, North Carolina.

Wilderness, followed a similar pattern. Nevertheless, Lee proved more than capable on the defensive.

From May 5-6, Lee's men won a tactical victory at the Battle of the Wilderness, which was fought so close to where the Battle of Chancellorsville took place a year earlier that soldiers encountered skeletons that had been buried in (too) shallow graves in 1863. Moreover, the woods were so thick that neither side could actually see who they were shooting at, and whole brigades at times got lost in the forest. Still, both armies sustained heavy casualties while Grant kept attempting to move the fighting to a setting more to his advantage, but the heavy forest made coordinated movements almost impossible.

Though ultimately one of the most horrendous battles of the war (where wounded men literally burned to death in fires ignited by rifle fire sparking the underbrush), by the end of the first day, Union forces still held control of vital intersections. That night, Grant ordered General Hancock and his Second Corps to "throw everything he had into an assault on the Confederate right at dawn."[23]

The next day, as Hancock rode up and down the line establishing order and preparing his men for battle, he was approached by Grant's personal aid, General Horace Porter, who later described the "knightly corps commander," writing, "His face was flushed with the excitement of victory, his eyes were lighten by the fire of battle, his flaxen hair was thrust back from his temples, his right are was extended to its full length in pointing out certain positions . . . his commanding form towered still higher as he rose in his stirrups to peer through the openings in the woods. It was enough to inspire the troops he led to deeds of unmatched heroism."[24] Clearly, Hancock was poised for a major victory.

Hancock's May 6, dawn assault initially went well, successful in driving Confederate forces back to Lee's command post a mile away. By one account, "in his wake along the line of his advance, the enemies dead were everywhere visible; his wounded strewn the road; prisoners had been captured, and battle-flags had been taken."[25] However, he wasn't the only one pressing an assault; Lee was determined to launch an attack in the same sector using Longstreet's corps. Longstreet ordered the advance of six brigades by heavy skirmish lines--four to flank the Union right and two against the front--which allowed his men to deliver continuous fire into the enemy while proving elusive targets themselves. After a confusing exchange of gunfire in a heavily-wooded area, Longstreet launched a powerful flanking attack along the Orange Plank Road against Hancock's II Corps that greatly surprised it and nearly drove it off the field.

[23]   McPherson, James M. *Ordeal by Fire: The Civil War and Reconstruction.* Page 448.
[24]   Porter, Horace. *Campaigning with Grant.* Pages 57--58.
[25]   Porter, Horace. *Campaigning with Grant.* Page 58.

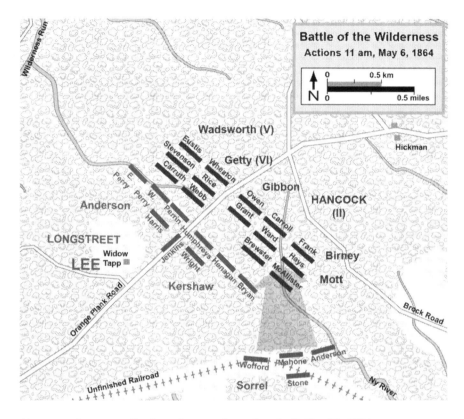

Battle of the Wilderness
Actions 11 am, May 6, 1864

Almost exactly a year earlier, just miles away from where the Battle of the Wilderness was fought, Stonewall Jackson was mortally wounded by fire from his own men. Longstreet nearly suffered the same fate. During the assault, Longstreet was himself wounded — accidentally shot by one of his own men – with the ball passing through the base of his neck and lodging in his shoulder. To assure his men, Longstreet raised his hat as he was being carried off the field, but with Longstreet incapacitated, the momentum of the attack was lost, forcing General Lee to delay further action until units could be realigned. This setback gave Hancock and his corps sufficient time to reorganize, and they were able to hold their position until night fell.

By the end of the day, the battle ended at virtually the same place it had started that morning, except now, thousands of men lay dead. Confederate General Edward Porter Alexander later spoke of the loss of Longstreet at the critical juncture of the battle, saying, "I have always believed that, but for Longstreet's fall, the panic which was fairly underway in Hancock's Corps would have been extended and have resulted in Grant's being forced to retreat back across the

Rapidan."[26]

The Confederates had won a tactical victory at a staggering cost, inflicting 17,000 casualties on Grant and suffering 11,000 of their own. Grant disengaged from the battle in the same position as Hooker before him at Chancellorsville, McClellan on the Virginian Peninsula, and Burnside after Fredericksburg. His men got the familiar dreadful feeling that they would retreat back across the Rapidan toward Washington, as they had too many times before. This time, however, Grant made the fateful decision to keep moving south, inspiring his men by telling them that he was prepared to "fight it out on this line if it takes all Summer."[27]

Using the Union V Corps under Major General Gouverneur K. Warren, Grant moved forward in a series of flanking maneuvers that continued to move the army steadily closer to Richmond. But Lee continued to parry each thrust. The next major battle took place at Spotsylvania Court House from May 8-21, with the heaviest fighting on May 12 when a salient in the Confederate line nearly spelled disaster for Lee's army.

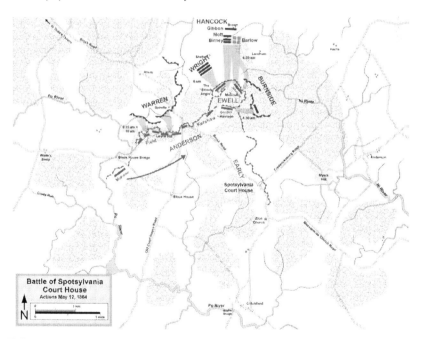

26   Alexander, Edward P. (Gallagher, Gary W. editor). *Fighting for the Confederacy: The Personal Recollections of General Edward Porter Alexander.* Page 360.
27   Fellman, Michael. *The Making of Robert E. Lee.* Page 167.

Under General Grant's direct orders, at 4:30 a.m. on May 12, 1864, Hancock's II Corps burst out through the rain and fog, leading a large-scale assault at Spotsylvania Court House that caught the Confederates completely by surprise. Breaking through Lee's front line at "the mule shoe" with relative ease, Hancock's corps effectively split the Confederate Army in half-- capturing approximately twenty guns and 2,800 prisoners in the process, the majority of General Jackson's legendary "Stonewall Brigade".

In their zeal, however, the Union forces lost their cohesion, allowing the Confederates to launch an exuberant counterattack that resulted in savage, unrelenting fighting in the rain lasting hours, while bodies piled up on both sides. (Men were literally trampled under the mud as soldiers advanced to take the place of their fallen comrades.) Fighting raged around the "Bloody Angle" for hours, with soldiers fighting hand to hand before the Confederates finally dislodged the Union soldiers. At midnight, the Confederates finally abandoned "Mule Shoe," but Grant had failed to break Lee's defenses as planned.

For the next two weeks, Grant pursued Lee, sending a number of his commanders to outmaneuver Lee's army; attempting to disrupt Lee's supply lines and threaten his rear, thus forcing him out of the trenches to fight, or further retreat.

Lee's army continued to stoutly defend against several attacks by the Army of the Potomac, but massive casualties were inflicted on both sides. After Spotsylvania, Grant had already incurred about 35,000 casualties while inflicting nearly 25,000 casualties on Lee's army. Grant, of course, had the advantage of a steady supply of manpower, so he could afford to fight the war of attrition. It was a fact greatly lost on the people of the North, however, who knew Grant's track record from Shiloh and saw massive casualty numbers during the Overland Campaign. Grant was routinely criticized as a butcher.

As fate would have it, the only time during the Overland Campaign Lee had a chance to take the initiative was after Spotsylvania. During the fighting that came to be known as the Battle of North Anna, Lee was heavily debilitated with illness. Grant nearly fell into Lee's trap by splitting his army in two along the North Anna before avoiding it.

By the time the two armies reached Cold Harbor near the end of May 1864, Grant incorrectly thought that Lee's army was on the verge of collapse. Though his frontal assaults had failed spectacularly at places like Vicksburg, Grant believed that Lee's army was on the ropes and could be knocked out with a strong attack. The problem was that Lee's men were now masterful at quickly constructing defensive fortifications, including earthworks and trenches that made their positions impregnable. While Civil War generals kept employing Napoleonic tactics, Civil War soldiers were building the types of defensive works that would be the harbinger of World War I's trench warfare.

Despite having not been "officially" condemned by Generals Lee or Longstreet for his role in the ill-fated "Pickett's Charge", Pickett's reputation quickly went into decline. Pickett's division was detached in support of General Lee's operation in the Overland Campaign just before the Battle of Cold Harbor, in which Pickett's division occupied the center of the defensive line, a position that did not come under direct Union attack.

On June 3, 1864, sensing he could break Lee's army, Grant ordered a full out assault at dawn in the hopes of catching the rebels before they could fully entrench. As fate had it, Hancock's men became part of the vanguard of an attack that would go down in history as one of the bloodiest and costliest failures of the War. Although the story of Union soldiers pinning their names on the back of their uniforms in anticipation of death at Cold Harbor is apocryphal, the frontal assault on June 3 inflicted thousands of Union casualties in about half an hour. In just minutes, 7,000 Union soldiers were killed or wounded as 30,000 Confederate soldiers successfully held the line against 50,000 Union troops, losing just 1,500 men in the process. Though credited with a valiant attempt, Hancock's efforts were overshadowed by Grant's horrendous failure and costly bad judgment.

With another 12,000 casualties at Cold Harbor, Grant had suffered about as many casualties in a month as Lee had in his entire army at the start of the campaign. Grant later admitted, "I have always regretted that the last assault at Cold Harbor was ever made...No advantage whatever was gained to compensate for the heavy loss we sustained."

Chapter 16: The Siege of Petersburg

Although Grant's results were widely condemned, he continued to push toward Richmond. After Cold Harbor, Grant managed to successfully steal an entire day's march on Lee and crossed the James River, attacking the Confederacy's primary railroad hub at Petersburg, which was only a few miles from Richmond. By the time Lee's army reached Petersburg, it had been defended by P.G.T. Beauregard, but now the Army of Northern Virginia had been pinned down at Petersburg. Grant knew that once Lee got wind that Union forces were on the move, he would send his best units to strengthen Petersburg lines. But as had happened several times before, Grant's generals hesitated to act, allowing Confederate general P. G. T. Beauregard to build new interior defenses by June 16. And even though Union forces were able to crack through Confederate lines by June 17, darkness fell before they could make on real inroads. The two armies dug in, and Grant prepared for a long term siege of the vital city.

During the Siege of Petersburg, Pickett commanded the Department of Southern Virginia and North Carolina over the winter months, and then served as a division commander in the defenses of Richmond. The siege would carry on for nearly 10 months, and during the siege the most famous battle took place when Union engineers burrowed underneath the Confederate siege lines and lit the fuse on a massive amount of ammunition, creating a "crater" in the field. But even then, the Battle of the Crater ended with a Union debacle, as Union forces swarmed into the crater instead of around it, giving the Confederates the ability to practically shoot fish in a barrel.

Still, by the beginning of 1865, the Confederacy was in utter disarray. The main Confederate army in the West under John Bell Hood had been nearly destroyed by General Thomas's men at the Battle of Franklin in late 1864, and Sherman's army faced little resistance as it marched through the Carolinas. Although Confederate leaders remained optimistic, by the summer of 1864 they had begun to consider desperate measures in an effort to turn around the war. From 1863-1865, Confederate leaders had even debated whether to conscript black slaves and enlist them as soldiers. Even as their fortunes looked bleak, the Confederates refused to issue an official policy to enlist blacks. It was likely too late to save the Confederacy anyway.

By the time Lincoln delivered his Second Inaugural Address in March 1865, the end of the war was in sight. That month, Lincoln famously met with Grant, Sherman, and Admiral David Porter at City Point, Grant's headquarters during the siege, to discuss how to handle the end of the war.

Chapter 17: Five Forks

The war was nearly over, but Pickett's most controversial battle had not yet taken place.

In late March of 1865, Union cavalryman General Phil Sheridan destroyed what was left of Confederate general Jubal Early's cavalry near Waynesborough, Virginia, and then moved 12,000 men into position at General Lee's right flank near the crossroads known as Five Forks, effectively threatening Lee's supply line. Knowing that without unfettered access to men and supplies both he and Richmond could not withstand the battle that was imminent, Lee sent what infantry and cavalrymen he could muster to hold Five Forks, including Pickett's troops.

On March 31, Pickett's men engaged Union general Phil Sheridan's forces, leading to an ultimate showdown the following day at Five Forks. When the Battle of Five Forks finally commenced, however, Pickett was two miles away, said to have been enjoying a shad bake with Generals Fitzhugh Lee and Thomas L. Rosser. Thus by the time he reached the battlefield, it was too late; Union troops had already overrun Pickett's defense lines. Historians have attributed it to unusual environmental acoustics that prevented Pickett and his staff from hearing the battle despite their close proximity, not that it mattered to the Confederates at the time.

The following day, battles raged across the siege lines of Petersburg, eventually spelling the doom for Lee's defenses. On April 2, 1865, Lee abandoned Petersburg, and thus Richmond with it. For Pickett, after the humiliating defeat at Gettysburg (which he survived because he was not himself on the battlefield), Five Forks was a final disgrace, but on a happier note, as General Grant was capturing Richmond, Pickett received a silver service from Union general George

McClellan and several other Union officers in acknowledgement of Pickett's wife Sallie having given birth to a son. The accompanying note said, "To our friend and classmate, George Pickett."[28] Sallie would also later write that Lincoln came to visit her after touring Richmond, but historians dispute that story.

Chapter 18: Appomattox

Lee's battered army began stumbling toward a rail depot in the hopes of avoiding being surrounded by Union forces and picking up much needed food rations. While Grant's army continued to chase Lee's retreating army westward, the Confederate government sought to escape across the Deep South. On April 4, President Lincoln entered Richmond and toured the home of Confederate President Jefferson Davis.

As historical records indicate, after the Battle of Five Forks, Pickett had few soldiers left to command. General Lee ordered Pickett and two other generals to transfer their remaining men to other units and return to base. While this order was regarded by many Confederate insiders as the logical reorganizational move in last-ditch efforts to muster a cohesive, resistant force, others saw it as reflective of Lee's disappointment in Pickett's performance at Gettysburg (and diminished capacity to command effectively). In either regard, the reasons behind Lee's decision would soon prove moot as Confederate forces faced their final attempts to defend their "cause."

Even today, historical debate continues as to whether or not Lee relieved Pickett of command after the Battle of Sayler's Creek (in which Pickett apparently did not participate) on April 6, 1865, or simply transferred his troops to other units. Lee's chief-of-staff, Lt. Colonel Walter H. Taylor, wrote after the War that he issued orders for Lee relieving Pickett (along with Maj. Generals Richard H. Anderson and Bushrod R. Johnson) but copies of such orders have never been recovered. In any regard, by some accounts, Pickett continued to command what remained of his division (now reduced in number to below that of a brigade), and is said to have reported to Longstreet—though Longstreet makes no mention of Pickett's division in his final report.

Fittingly, the food rations Lee moved toward did not arrive as anticipated. On April 7, 1865, Grant sent Lee the first official letter demanding Lee's surrender. In it Grant wrote, "The results of the last week must convince you of the hopelessness of further resistance on the part of the Army of Northern Virginia in this struggle. I feel it is so, and regret it as my duty to shift myself from the responsibility of any further effusion of blood by asking of you the surrender of that portion of the Confederate States army known as the Army of Northern Virginia."[29] Passing the note to General Longstreet, now his only advisor, Longstreet said, "Not yet."[30] But by the

---

[28] Gaffney, P. and D. Gaffney. *The Civil War: Exploring History One Week at a Time*. Page 84.

[29] Horn, Stanley F. (editor). *The Robert E. Lee Reader*. Page 436.

following evening during what would be the final Confederate Council of War (and after one final attempt had been made to break through Union lines), Lee finally succumbed, stating regretfully, "There is nothing left me but to go and see General Grant, and I had rather die a thousand deaths."[31]

Communications continued until April 9, at which point Lee and Grant two met at Appomattox Court House. When Lee and Grant met, the styles in dress captured the personality differences perfectly. Lee was in full military attire, while Grant showed up casually in a muddy uniform. The Civil War's two most celebrated generals were meeting for the first time since the Mexican-American War.

The McLean Parlor in Appomattox Court House. McLean's house was famously fought around during the First Battle of Bull Run, leading him to move to Appomattox.

On April 9, Pickett is thought to have commanded his remaining troops in the Battle of Appomattox Courthouse, forming the final battle line of the Army of Northern Virginia until its defeat. The Confederate soldiers had continued fighting while Lee worked out the terms of surrender, and they were understandably devastated to learn that they had surrendered. Some of his men had famously suggested to Lee that they continue to fight on. Porter Alexander would later rue the fact that he suggested to Lee that they engage in guerrilla warfare, which earned him a stern rebuke from Lee. As a choked-up Lee rode down the troop line on his famous horse Traveller that day, he addressed his defeated army, saying, "Men, we have fought through the

30   Davis, Kenneth C. *The Civil War: Everything You Need to Know About America's Greatest Conflict but Never Learned.* Page 402.
31   Davis, Kenneth C. *The Civil War: Everything You Need to Know About America's Greatest Conflict but Never Learned.* Page 402.

war together. I have done my best for you; my heart is too full to say more." Later that day, Pickett surrendered the 800 men under his command.

Appomattox is frequently cited as the end of the Civil War, but there still remained several Confederate armies across the country, mostly under the command of General Joseph E. Johnston, who Lee had replaced nearly 3 years earlier. On April 26, Johnston surrendered all of his forces to General Sherman. Over the next month, the remaining Confederate forces would surrender or quit. The last skirmish between the two sides took place May 12-13, ending ironically with a Confederate victory at the Battle of Palmito Ranch in Texas. Two days earlier, Jefferson Davis had been captured in Georgia.

Although the surrender of the Army of Northern Virginia to General Ulysses S. Grant and the Army of the Potomac at Appomattox Courthouse did not officially end the long and bloody Civil War, the surrender is often considered the final chapter of the war. For that reason, Appomattox has captured the popular imagination of Americans ever since Lee's surrender there on April 9, 1865.

Chapter 19: Post-Civil War Years

Personal Life, Final Years

After the Civil War, despite being paroled, Pickett fled to Canada to avoid prosecution for "war crimes", notably the mistreatment and execution of Union prisoners-of-war while he was commanding in North Carolina, and like many other former Confederate officers who had been West Point graduates but resigned their commissions at the start of the Civil War, Pickett had difficulty obtaining amnesty after the War's end. Though former Union officers (including Ulysses S. Grant) supported pardoning Pickett, it wasn't until U. S. House Resolution 3086 "which would act to remove the political disabilities of George E. Pickett of Virginia" was passed by Congress on June 23, 1874 (just one year before his death) that he was granted a full pardon.

Returning to Norfolk, Virginia in 1866, Pickett declined political appointments from old military friends and colleagues, an offer of a commission as a general in the Egyptian army, as well as an offer from Ulysses S. Grant to become a United States Marshall, accepting instead a position heading the Virginia branch of the New York Insurance Company (overseeing agencies in Virginia, North Carolina, and West Virginia). Some sources list the Washington Life Insurance Company as his place of employment, citing that during his employment, he and his wife and sons lived at the Exchange Hotel located on the east side of 14th Street between Main and Franklin Streets in Richmond.

George Edward Pickett died in Norfolk, Virginia on July 30, 1875 at the age of fifty, and was buried in Richmond's Hollywood Cemetery. History records a number of possible causes of death, none apparently substantiated. He (and later his wife Sallie) was buried in a grave marked with an elaborate memorial in Hollywood Cemetery on South Cherry Street in Richmond, Virginia. Commissioned in 1875 by a group of veterans from his division calling themselves the "Pickett Division Association," the memorial was originally intended to be placed at Gettysburg National Military Park at the "High Water Mark of Pickett's Charge," but was erected instead in Richmond when the U. S. War Department refused permission to have it established on the battlefield.

Pickett's grave at Hollywood Cemetery

A monument to Pickett also stands in the American Camp on San Juan Island, Washington, erected by the Washington University Historical Society on October 21, 1904 in honor of his work while stationed there.

Fort Pickett, in Blackstone, Virginia, is named in Pickett's honor. Originally a site for the Civilian Conservation Corps (CCC Corps), it was an active U. S. Army training facility during World War II and is currently occupied by the Virginia National Guard.

In February of 1943, the Todd-Houston Shipbuilding Corporation in Houston, Texas built a liberty ship named the SS George E. Pickett, an EC2-S-C1-type officially launched on March 31, 1943. However, like all liberty ships that survived World War II, the SS George E. Pickett was scrapped in 1969.

Chapter 20: Pickett's Legacy

Overview

Based on accounts of his days at West Point Military Academy and later war records, it is generally accepted that most everyone found George Edward Pickett likable, and he was regarded as one of the most affable officers in the Army of Northern Virginia. With the accolades "dapper" and "dashing" frequently used to describe him, he is said to have cultivated a gregarious, "swashbuckling" image that many found appealing.

While history often characterizes George Pickett's place in American history as hinging on a single assault which occurred on the afternoon of July 3, 1863 at Gettysburg, Pennsylvania, which from many perspectives spelled the beginning of the end for the Confederate "Cause", it would be more accurate to say that it was by virtue of that fateful attack being *labeled* "Pickett's Charge" that his name was pushed to the forefront of Civil War history. Indeed, had the charge been named "Lee's Charge" or "Longstreet's Charge"--which would have been equally if not more appropriate—Pickett the man may have ended up little more than a footnote in Civil War annals, mostly owing to the fact that he was the only division commander to not suffer injury during the charge. Thus, much speculation surrounds exactly *why* Pickett is survived by this dubious recognition.

By some accounts, it was General Lee's choice to designate Pickett as "leading the charge" that had at least initially led to the press mistakenly attributing the battle plan to Pickett. In the field, however, Pickett clearly did not see the planned attack as such when he wrote to his wife just before the battle, "If Old Peter's (Longstreet) nod (to attack) means death, goodbye and God bless you little one."[32] And in actuality, Pickett was just one of three generals who led the

---

[32] Lanning, Michael Lee. *The Civil War 100.* Page 328.

charge, following Longstreet's orders.

Some historians attribute the subsequent attention to Pickett to the Virginian newspapers who praised Pickett's Virginia division for making the most progress during the charge, thereby using Pickett's *comparative* success as a means of criticizing the actions of the other states' troops who did not advance as far. After all, it was men of Pickett's division who were able to reach and breach the Union line on the ridge, with Armistead's brigade making the furthest progress through Union lines.

While Pickett's charge at the Battle of Gettysburg is considered one of the great moments in American history (its failure decisively ending the battle), history does not record the life of George Pickett *per se,* as much as it documents his participation at Gettysburg – and specifically, the "Charge" that bears his name to this day. Although the charge itself is regarded as the high tide of the "Confederate Cause," the failure of the battle effectively shattered and demoralized the Army of Northern Virginia, which never regained its earlier power or sense of invincibility.

As history reflects, apart from Pickett's "charge," although his War record was honorable and meritorious, there were dozens of other unsung (and perhaps more deserving) division commanders on both sides of the War who received little or no recognition whatsoever. In short, George Pickett is remembered more for his fame (or infamy, depending on perspective) than his military effectiveness.

On "Her Soldier"

Decades after George Pickett's death, his widow Sallie became a well-known writer and public speaker on "her Soldier", which eventually lead to what many historians consider the *idealized* Pickett (the perfect Southern gentleman and soldier), as well as considerable controversy regarding Sallie's method of exalting her husband.

Two books published posthumously under Pickett's name, *The Heart of a Soldier, As Revealed in the Intimate Letters of Gen'l George E. Pickett* (published in 1913) and *Soldier of the South: General Pickett's War Letters to His Wife* (published in 1928), are assumed to have been written and edited by Sallie, and thus subsequently characterized as "unreliable works that were fictionalized by Pickett's wife."[33] Sallie herself authored *Pickett and His Men* (published in 1913), ultimately resulting in Pickett's true deeds largely obscured by the so-called "Lost Cause" mythology she promoted.

Historian John C. Waugh describes George Pickett as "an excellent brigade commander, he never proved he could handle a division," then quotes Pickett friend Union general George B.

---

[33] Eicher, John H., and David J. Eicher. *Civil War High Commands.* Page 429.

McClellan as saying: "Perhaps there is no doubt that he was the best infantry soldier developed on either side during the Civil War."[34] This quote was provided by Sallie Pickett in *The Heart of a Soldier* and is therefore deemed questionable in authenticity.

Controversy

By some accounts, George Pickett lamented to his dying day the great losses his men suffered at Gettysburg. Late in his life, Colonel John Mosby (who served under General J. E. B. Stuart but had no direct interaction with Robert E. Lee to draw from) claimed to have observed an interaction between Lee and Pickett that he characterized as "cold and reserved." However, others present at this meeting refuted this depiction, stating that Lee acted in his usual "reserved, gentlemanly fashion." Mosby further claimed that after their meeting, Pickett uttered bitterly "That man destroyed my division!"[35] However, many historians find Mosby's description of the encounter unlikely, based on numerous accounts describing Lee's temperament and demeanor both privately and with his men, and particularly with Pickett on record as having addressed the failure of "Pickett's Charge" by saying, "I've always thought the Yankees had something to do with it."[36]

The controversy surrounding Pickett's decision to capture and execute prisoners-of-war during his North Carolina (New Bern) Campaign is an issue that for many historians remains unresolved. In recent decades, some historians have attributed his decision to execute (rather than simply detain) the New Bern prisoners to declining mental health resulting from his disastrous show at Gettysburg and the subsequent fall from repute that followed. Some cite a letter written to his wife the day after the infamous battle in which he wrote, "Well, it is all over now. The battle is lost, and many of us are prisoners, many are dead, many wounded, bleeding, dying. Your soldier lives and mourns and but for you, my darling, he would rather, a million times rather, be back there with his dead, to sleep for all time in an unknown grave."[37]

Pickett proponents, however, offer a "more reasonable explanation" for his decisions at New Bern, contending that Pickett's actions were not the actions of a man in the final throes of emotional crisis (and professional decline), but a man exhibiting the rational behavior of a "sorely-tried commander" contending with one of the fundamental realities of field command--

---

[34] Waugh, John C. *The Class of 1846: From West Point to Appomattox: Stonewall Jackson, George McClellan, and Their Brothers.* Page 507.

[35] Tagg, Larry. *The Generals of Gettysburg.* Page 240.

[36] Boritt, Gabor S., ed. *Why the Confederacy Lost.* Page 19.

[37] Lanning, Michael Lee. *The Civil War 100.* Page 328.

the maintenance of his army in light of diminishing numbers. In keeping with Confederate concerns over desertion in North Carolina -- and General Lee's expressed desires -- Pickett intended to set an example that might deter the flow of desertion. As his supporters contend, after nearly three years fighting for the so-called "Southern Cause," Pickett no doubt found even the *thought* of desertion — with tens of thousands of men having already died for the Confederacy — increasingly deplorable.

In Pop Culture

Today, George Edward Pickett is widely perceived as a tragic hero of sorts a flamboyant "dandy" of an officer who desperately wanted to lead his troops into a glorious battle but was repeatedly robbed of the opportunity, until the disastrous charge at the Battle of Gettysburg that was doomed from the start. Douglas Southall Freeman, best known for his multi-volume biographies of Robert E. Lee and George Washington, did much to enhance Pickett's reputation in popular culture with *Lee's Lieutenants* (published in 1944), as did Michael Shaara with his novel *The Killer Angels* (published in 1975) and the film based off of it, *Gettysburg* (1993). At the same time, these also served to further obscure the real Pickett and his accomplishments in the Civil War.

In the 1993 film *Gettysburg* (based on Shaara's *The Killer Angels*), actor Stephen Lang portrays General George Pickett, and in the 2003 *Gettysburg* prequel *Gods and Generals* (also based on a novel by Jeffrey Shaara) set in the time prior to the Battle of Gettysburg, Pickett is portrayed by actor Billy Campbell.

Accounts of Pickett's Charge

PETTIGREW'S CHARGE AT GETTYSBURG

By General B. D. Fry.

In the numerous accounts of the battle of Gettysburg heretofore published, the writers have generally referred to the last effort made by the Confederate troops as "Pickett's charge," and in almost every instance have conveyed the idea that no troops but Pickett's division took an active part in that fierce and tremendous struggle. Disclaiming any intention to detract in the least from the glory won on that day by the gallant Virginia division, or its heroic commander, who had then been for more than twenty years one of my most valued friends, I may be permitted to say that some injustice has been done to the division commanded by General Pettigrew.

As colonel of the Thirteenth Alabama infantry, I was attached to Archer's brigade of Heth's division. That brigade opened the battle on the morning of July 1st, and during the fighting which immediately ensued General Heth was wounded, and the command of the division devolved upon Brigadier-General Pettigrew. General Archer was captured, and I succeeded him in command of the brigade.

During the forenoon of the 3d, while our division was resting in line behind the ridge and skirt of woods which masked us from the enemy, Generals Lee, Longstreet and A. P. Hill rode up, and, dismounting, seated themselves on the trunk of a fallen tree some fifty or sixty paces from where I sat on my horse at the right of our division. After an apparently careful examination of a map, and a consultation of some length, they remounted and rode away. Staff officers and couriers began to move briskly about, and a few minutes after General Pettigrew rode up and informed me that after a heavy cannonade we would assault the position in our front, and added: "They will of course return the fire with all the guns they have; we must shelter the men as best we can, and make them lie down." At the same time he directed me to see General Pickett at once and have an understanding as to the dress in the advance. I rode to General Pickett, whose division was formed on the right of and in line with ours. He appeared to be in excellent spirits, and, after a cordial greeting and a pleasant reference to our having been together in work of that kind at Chapultipec, expressed great confidence in the ability of our troops to drive the enemy after they had been "demoralized by our artillery." General Garnett, who commanded his left brigade, having joined us, it was agreed that he would dress on my command. I immediately returned and informed General Pettigrew of this agreement. It was then understood that my command should be considered the centre, and that in the assault both divisions should allign themselves by it. Soon after the two divisions moved forward about a hundred paces, and the men lay down behind our line of batteries. The cannonade which followed has been often and justly described as the most terrible of the war. In it my command suffered a considerable loss. Several officers were killed and wounded, with a number of the rank and file. I received a painful wound on the right shoulder from a fragment of shell. After lying inactive under that deadly storm of hissing and exploding missiles, it seemed a relief to go forward to the desperate assault. At a signal from Pettigrew I called my command to attention. The men sprang up with cheerful alacrity, and the long line advanced. "Stormed at with shot and shell," it moved steadily on, and even when grape, canister, and musket balls began to rain upon it the gaps were quickly closed and the allignment preserved. Strong as was the position of the enemy, it seemed that such determination could not fail. I heard Garnett give a command to his men which, amid the rattle of musketry, I could not distinguish. Seeing my look or gesture of inquiry, he called our, "I am dressing on you!" A few seconds after he fell dead. A moment later- and after Captain Williams and Colonel George had been wounded by my side- a shot through the thigh prostrated me. I was so confident of victory that to some of my men who ran up to carry me off I shouted, "Go on; it will not last five minutes longer!" The men rushed forward into the smoke, which soon became so dense that I could see little of what was going on before me. But a moment later I heard General Pettigrew, behind me, calling to some of his staff to "rally them on the left." The roll of musketry was then incessant, and I believe that the Federal troops- probably blinded by the smoke- continued a rapid fire for some minutes after none but dead and wounded remained in their front. At length the firing ceased, and cheer after cheer from the enemy announced the failure of our attack. I was of course left a prisoner.

As evidence of how close was the fighting at that part of the line, I saw a Federal soldier with an ugly wound in his shoulder, which he told me he received from the spear on the end of one of my regimental colors; and I remembered having that morning observed and laughingly commented on the fact that the color-bearer of the Thirteenth Alabama had attached to his staff a formidable-looking lance head. All of the five regimental colors of my command reached the line of the enemy's works, and many of my men and officers were killed or wounded after passing over it. I believe the same was true of other brigades in General Pettigrew's command.

It is probable that Pickett's division, which up to that time had taken no part in the battle, was mainly relied upon for the final assault; but whatever may have been the first plan of attack, the division under Pettigrew went into it as part of the line of battle, and from the commencement of the advance to the closing death grapple, his right brigade was the directing one. General Pettigrew, who I know was that day in the thickest of the fire, was killed in a skirmish a few days later. No more earnest and gallant officer served in the Confederate army.

B. D. Fry.

Montgomery, Alabama, December 14th, 1878.

(Source: Southern Historical Society Papers, Vol.7, p91-93)

ARMISTEAD AT THE BATTLE OF GETTYSBURG.

Extracts from Letters Written by Dr. R. W. Martin to

Rev. JAMES POINDEXTER.

When Armistead's Brigade was in line of battle a short time before the advance was ordered, the general marched up and down in front of his troops encouraging them in every way and said these words: "Men, remember what you are fighting for. Remember your homes, your firesides, your wives, mothers, sisters and your sweethearts."

When the signal guns were fired Armistead instantly called attention, and instantly every man was on his feet. After a few words he walked to the front of the Fifty-third Virginia Regiment, his battalion of direction, and addressed the color bearer, "Sergeant, are you going to put those colors on the enemy's works over yonder?"

"Yes, general, if mortal man can do it."

He then exhorted the men to follow their colors and to remember the brave words of their color bearer.

When the advance commenced Armistead placed himself in front of the colors of the Fifty-third Regiment, and from that point watched and directed the advance until within a short distance of the enemy's line. When approximating the advance line General Kemper rode up to him and said, "General, hurry up, my men can stand no more."

He quietly turned to the officer commanding his battalion of direction and said, "Colonel, double quick." The double quick soon quickened into a run, the run into a charge, Armistead all the time in front of his line of battle, and when the desperate effort came and the final rush for the rock fence was made he dew his sword, put his hat on the end of it, called upon his men to follow, rushed over the rock fence and was shot just as he reached the enemy's guns between the two lines in the bloody angle, thus sealing with his life's blood the high water mark of the rebellion.

As Armistead was carried from the field he met Hancock as he was hurrying to the front. They recognized each other, and Hancock dismounted and grasped his hand and told him how sorry he was to see him wounded. Armistead returned his kindly expression and told him the wound was mortal and that he had on his person some things that he wish to entrust to him to be returned when opportunity presented to his people in Virginia. Hancock accepted the commission and tried to persuade Armistead to look upon the bright side, that he probably was not so seriously hurt as he feared, excused himself by saying he was compelled to hurry to the front, left Armistead, promising to see him the next day. In a short time he was wounded himself and they never met again.

This was related to me as I lay on the ground back of the battle line where hundreds of wounded were carried after the fight, by one of Hancock's staff, who rode up just about dusk and found a number of men congregated about me. When he found I was a badly wounded "Johnny Reb" Colonel he dismounted, drove everybody away that I might have fresh air, and commenced a conversation.

When he found that I was of Armistead's Brigade, he said, "Armistead, Armistead. I have just left him, he is mortally wounded," and then related the above, and said, "I will have you taken care of," etc.

Armistead lingered through the 4th and died on the 5th, leaving an example of patriotism, heroism and devotion to duty which ought to be handed down through the ages.

Here's my heart and hand.

Sincerely and truly,

R. W. Martin,

Pittsylvania Tribune.

(Source: Southern Historical Society Papers, Vol. 39, pp. 186-187)

[From the Richmond, Va., Dispatch, January 26, 1896.]

GETTYSBURG CHARGE.

————

Paper as to Pickett's Men.

————

[The following is a compilation of a modest infantryman. Captain Martin W. Hazlewood is an earnest member of the History Committee of the Grand Camp of Confederate Veterans, Virginia.-ED.]

This interesting paper on the "Gettysburg Charge," was read before Pickett Camp Monday night, January 20th, by Captain M. W. Hazlewood:

The third day's battle of Gettysburg, more familiarly spoken of as 'Pickett's charge," has been so often treated in books and essays, that it would seem almost useless to write on the subject at this late day. In defense of the commanding general, whose conduct has been unwittingly impeached by superficial writers in search of a scapegoat for the untoward results of this fatal battle, and in justice to the troops engaged, it will hardly be regarded as out of place to cite some facts which have not ordinarily attracted attention.

On the morning of the 3d of July the Federal line was complete, and occupied all the hills and ridges from Culp's Hill to Round Top mountain, without a break, while Kilpatrick's cavalry enveloped the Confederate right, where McLaws and Hood, with about eight thousand men, were confronted by the Fifth and Sixth army corps occupying an impregnable position. These facts, it would seem, decided General Lee to form a column of attack on the point where Wright's Brigade had penetrated the Federal line on the previous evening.

AN INTERVIEW WITH LEE.

On the night Of July 3d, General Imboden states that in response to a message he had an interview with General Lee, during which the latter, in a voice tremulous with emotion, said:

"I never saw troops behave more magnificently than Pickett's Division of Virginians did to-day in that grand charge upon the enemy. And if they had been supported as they were to have been-- but, for some reason not yet fully explained to me, were not--we would have held the position and the day would have been ours."

This remark of the commanding general has been almost universally construed as a censure of Heth's and Pender's troops; but this is as unjustifiable as it is untrue. General Lee's official report was forwarded to the War Department January 20, 1864, more than six months after the battle, and there is not a word in that report which reflects on these troops.

THE LINE OF BATTLE.

General Lee gives the order of line of battle as follows:

"General Longstreet ordered forward the column of attack, consisting of Pickett's and Heth's Divisions, in two lines, Pickett's on the right, Wilcox's Brigade marched in rear of Pickett's right, to guard that flank, and Heth's was supported by Lane's and Scales's Brigades, under General Trimble."

General Longstreet in his report says: "Pickett's Division was arranged, two brigades in the front line, supported by his third brigade, and Wilcox's Brigade was ordered to move in rear of his right flank, to protect it from any force that the enemy might attempt to move against it. Heth's Division, under the command of Brigadier-General Pettigrew, was arranged in two lines, and these supported by part of Major-General Pender's Division, under Major-General Trimble. * * * *About 2 P. M. General Pickett, who had been charged with the duty of arranging the lines behind our batteries, reported that the troops were in order."

It will thus be seen that Heth's Division was a part of the column of attack, and must not be regarded as a mere support to Pickett.

General Lee further says: "The batteries were directed to be pushed forward as the infantry progressed, protect their flanks, and support their attacks closely."

These excerpts enable us to give a diagram of the column of attack, as it should have appeared in accordance with the foregoing orders, when it advanced, to which is added Anderson's three Brigades, which, as will appear further on, was to be a part of the supporting column._____

FRONT.

RIGHT

LEFT

....0..0..0..0..0..0..0..0

....Nine Howitzers.

Pettigrew.................Archer..............Garnett.............Kemper.

Brockenbrough............Davis......................Armistead..............

Lane..............Scales..Perry..............Wilcox.

Wright..........Posey..........Mahone..

McIntosh...Lane...Garnett...Pegram...Poague...Cabell...Dearing...Eshleman...Alexander...Henry

.

REAR.

WAS A FORLORN HOPE.

The strength of this formation can be readily apprehended. With a compact triple line of infantry, supported by some twenty or more batteries, commanded by Colonel E. P. Alexander, masked in what was virtually one battery, the shock must have been overwhelming. In addition, General Pendleton had placed at the disposal of Colonel Alexander nine howitzers, belonging to Hill's Corps, with which Alexander says he intended to precede the infantry, but when sent for they could not be found, some having been removed by order of General Pendleton, and others had changed their position to avoid the shelling. By comparing the following diagram, which represents the advance as it was made, with the preceding diagram, it will be realized at a glance that "Pickett's charge" was, indeed, a forlorn hope.

EAST.

Brockenbrough....Davis....Pettigrew....Archer....Garnett....Kemper.

.... Lane............Scales.............Armistead.........

0...0...0...0...0......................

.Major Eshleman's...................

five guns.........................

INFANTRY THAT TOOK PART.

The infantry actually engaged in this memorable conflict are as follows:

Pickett's Division --Kemper's Brigade--First, Third, Seventh, Eleventh, and Twenty-fourth Virginia Regiments. Garnett's Brigade--Eighth, Eighteenth, Nineteenth, Twenty-eighth and Fifty-sixth Virginia Regiments. Armistead's Brigade--Ninth, Fourteenth, Thirty-eighth, and Fifty-seventh Virginia Regiments.

Heth's Division --Archer's Brigade--Thirteenth Alabama Regiment and Fifth Alabama Battalion, and the First, Seventh, and Fourteenth Tennessee Regiments. Pettigrew's Brigade-- Eleventh, Twenty-sixth, Forty-seventh, and Fifty-second North Carolina Regiments. Davis' Brigade--Second, Eleventh, and Forty-second Mississippi, and Fifty-fifth North Carolina Regiments. Brockenbrough's Brigade--Fortieth, Forty-seventh, and Fifty-fifth Regiments, and the Twenty-second Virginia Battalion.

Pender's Division --Scales' Brigade--Thirteenth, Sixteenth, Twenty-second, Thirty-fourth, and Thirty-ninth North Carolina Regiments. Lane's Brigade--Seventh, Eighteenth, Twenty-eighth, Thirty-third and Thirty-seventh North Carolina Regiments.

Archer's was made the directing brigade of the line of battle.

BEYOND THE STONE WALL.

All these troops, numbering not more than 14,000, had, with the exception of Pickett's Division, been heavily engaged in the battle of the first of July. Brockenbrough's and Davis's Brigades, with absolutely no supports on the left or rear, unable to stand the tempest of shot and shell, gave way first. Pettigrew's Brigade dashed on, and, when within a short distance of the stone wall, a flanking column on the left poured in a destructive fire of musketry, causing what was left of the brigade to fall back. Archer's Brigade reached nearly, if not quite, the stone wall. From this point they retired to their former position on Seminary Ridge, passing through in a disorderly mass, and necessarily demoralizing to some extent the brigades of Lane and Scales, which continued to advance, however, some of the men reaching within a few yards of the stone wall; but none of the troops, except Pickett's, passed beyond the wall.

A Federal authority says: "Alexander Hays had several regiments well to the front behind stone walls, and on his extreme right was Woodruff's Battery of light twelves. Whether the fire was closer here, or whether, as some claim, the troops in Pettigrew's command were not as well seasoned to war as Pickett's men, it is certain that the attack on Hays was speedily repulsed. That it was pressed with resolution was attested by the dead and wounded on the field, which were as numerous in Hays's front as on any other part of it."

In the published records it is shown that medals were voted by Congress to Federal soldiers for flags captured from Pettigrew's, Archer's, and Scales's Brigades, every regiment in Archer's having lost their colors. The devotion and gallantry of the troops forming the left wing of Pickett's charge cannot justly be questioned.

ORDERS THROUGH THREE COURIERS.

The rear and flank of Pickett's Division was to have been supported by Wilcox and Perry, but there is good reason for supposing that they did not advance until after the attack had been repulsed. From General Wilcox's report we learn that about twenty or thirty minutes after Pickett's advance three different couriers came with orders to advance--one of them from Major-General Anderson,. probably a mile distant, to the left. General Wilcox adds: "Not a man of the division that I was ordered to support could I see."

Colonel Lang, commanding Perry's Brigade, says: "Soon after General Pickett's troops retired behind our position General Wilcox began to advance, and, in accordance with previous orders to conform to his movements, I moved forward also."

Colonel Alexander, in an article published since the war, says: "Wilcox's Brigade passed by us, moving to Pickett's support. There was no longer anything to support, and, with the keenest pity at the useless waste of life, I saw them advance. The men as they passed us looked bewildered, as if they wondered what they were expected to do, or why they were there. However, they were soon halted and moved back."

General Anderson, with the remaining brigades of his division--Wright, Posey, and Mahone--was expected to support the left wing of the column of attack. General A. P. Hill, his corps commander, says: "Anderson had been directed to hold his division ready to take advantage of any success which might be gained by the assaulting column, or to support it, if necessary."

General Anderson says: "I received orders to hold my division in readiness to move up in support, if it should become necessary."

General Longstreet says: "Major-General Anderson's Division was ordered forward to support and assist the wavering columns of Pettigrew and Trimble."

Anderson did not advance for the reason assigned by himself: "At what I supposed to be the proper time I was about to move forward Wright's and Posey's brigades, when Lieutenant-General Longstreet directed me to stop the movement, adding that it was useless, and would only involve unnecessary loss, the assault having failed."

PICKETT'S REPORT DESTROYED.

Who was responsible for the defective formation will probably never be known. General Pickett's report was suppressed in compliance with the suggestion contained in the following letter:

General George E. Pickett, Commanding, &c.:

General,--You and your men have crowned yourselves with glory; but we have the enemy to fight, and must carefully, at this critical moment, guard against dissensions, which the reflections in your report would create. I will therefore suggest that you destroy both copy and original, substituting one confined to casualties merely. I hope all will yet be well. I am, with respect,

Your obedient servant,

R. E. Lee, General.

Colonel Walter Harrison, assistant adjutant and inspector-general of Pickett's Division, in "Pickett's Men," published in 1870, says that "the two other divisions (Heth and Pender) were to move simultaneously in support, charging in second and third lines." This indicates that there was some idea of a triple line at Pickett's headquarters, though Colonel Harrison's narrative of the battle in this and other respects is somewhat faulty.

ORDERS MISUNDERSTOOD.

General Pettigrew was killed a few days after the battle, and made no report of his division. The reasonable inference is that the orders were misunderstood. The fact still remains, however, that five brigades did not advance to the support of the attacking column, and the left of

Pettigrew's line was wholly unsupported.

But there were other and most essential supports ordered to accompany Pickett's advance. General Lee's report, as before quoted, says: "The batteries were directed to be pushed forward as the infantry progressed, protect their flanks, and support their attacks closely."

General Longstreet says: "I gave orders for the batteries to refill their ammunition-chests, and to be prepared to follow up the advance of the infantry."

Major Eshleman reports: "It having been understood by a previous arrangement that the artillery should advance with the infantry, I immediately directed Captain Miller to advance his and Lieutenant Battle's batteries. Captain Miller, having suffered severely from the loss of men and horses, could move forward only three pieces of his own battery and one of Lieutenant Battle's section. Then, with one piece of Major Henry's battalion, under the direction of Major Haskell, he took position 400 or 500 yards to the front, and opened with deadly effect upon the enemy. With the exception of these five guns no others advanced."

GENERAL PENDLETON'S EXPLANATION.

The chief of artillery, General W. N. Pendleton, gives this explanation of the failure of the artillery to support the attacking column:

"Proceeding again to the right, to see about the anticipated advance of the artillery, delayed beyond expectation, I found, among other difficulties, many batteries getting out or low in ammunition, and the all-important question of supply received my earnest attention.

"Frequent shell endangering the first corps ordnance-train in the convenient locality I had assigned it, it had been removed farther back. This necessitated longer time for refilling caissons. What was worse, the train itself was very limited, so that its stock was soon exhausted, rendering requisite demands upon the reserve-train, farther off. The whole amount was thus being rapidly reduced. With our means to keep up supply at the rate required for such a conflict, proved practically impossible. There had to be, therefore, some relaxation of the protracted fire, and some lack of support for the deferred and attempted advance."

WHAT GENERAL LEE SAID.

This statement is relieved of its ambiguity by General Lee, who tells the result as follows:

"The troops moved steadily on, under a heavy fire of musketry and artillery, the main attack being directed against the enemy's left centre. His batteries reopened as soon as they appeared. Our own having nearly exhausted their ammunition in the protracted cannonade that preceded the infantry, were unable to reply, or render the necessary support to the attacking party. Owing to this fact, which was unknown to me when the assault took place, the enemy was enabled to throw a strong force of infantry against our left, already wavering under a concentrated fire of artillery from the ridge in front, and from Cemetery Hill on the left. It finally gave way, and the right, after penetrating the enemy's lines, entering his advance works, and capturing some of his artillery, was attacked simultaneously in front and on both flanks, and driven back with heavy loss."

There is no obscurity in the language of General Lee. The artillery did not render the necessary support, and, in consequence of this fact, the assault was a disastrous failure. This must be regarded as a complete vindication of the infantry. No blame can be attached to the officers and men of the artillery service participating in this fearful battle. They did their work nobly.

IS NO IDLE BOAST.

Taking into consideration the facts referred to in this paper, nearly all of which are from the official records, it will be seen that it was no vain boast of General Lee when he said of "Pickett's charge": "If they had been supported, as they were to have been, we would have held the position, and the day would have been ours."

It is perfectly apparent that General Lee attributed the defeat of Pickett solely to the failure of the batteries to advance as ordered; and it is equally certain that had the General been informed of the fact that the supply of ammunition was exhausted, the advance would not have been made at all.

(Source: Southern Historical Society Papers, Vol. 23, pages 229-237)

GETTYSBURG--PICKETT'S CHARGE.

Address by James F. Crocker, Before Stonewall Camp

Confederate Veterans, Portsmouth, Va., November 7, 1894.

_____

You command me to renew an inexpressible sorrow,

and to speak of those things of which we were a part.

_____

It is now nearly thirty years since there died away on the plains of Appomattox the sound of musketry and the roar of artillery. Then and there closed a struggle as heroic as ever was made by a brave and patriotic people for home government and home nationality. The tragic story of that great struggle has ever since been to me as a sealed, sacred book. I have never had the heart to open it. I knew that within its lids there were annals that surpassed the annals of all past times, in the intelligent, profound, and all-absorbing patriotism of our people--in the unselfish and untiring devotion of an entire population to a sacred cause--and in the brilliancy and prowess of arms which have shed an imperishable glory and honor on the people of this Southland. Yet there was such an ending to such great deeds! The heart of this great people, broken with sorrow, has watered with its tears those brilliant annals until every page shows the signs of a nation's grief. And with it all there are buried memories as dear and as sacred as the ashes of loved ones. No, I have had no heart to open the pages of that sacred yet tragic history. Not until you assigned me the duty of saying something of Pickett's charge at the battle of Gettysburg have I ever read the official or other accounts of that great battle; and when I later read them my heart bled afresh, and my inward being was shaken to the deepest depths of sad, tearful emotions, and I wished that you had given to another the task you gave to me.

On the 13th day of December, 1862, Burnside lead his great and splendidly equipped army down from the heights of Fredericksburg, crossed the Rappahannock, and gave battle to Lee. His army was repulsed with great slaughter and was driven back bleeding and mangled to its place of safety. The star of Burnside went down and out. General Hooker was called to the command of the Army of the Potomac. After five months of recuperation and convalescence, with greatly augmented numbers and with every appliance that military art and national wealth could furnish in the perfect equipment of a great army, it was proclaimed with much flourish amidst elated hopes and expectancy, that his army was ready to move. To meet this great host Lee could rely for success only on the great art of war and the unfailing courage of his soldiers. Hooker crossed the Rappahannock and commenced to entrench himself. Lee did not wait to be attacked, but at once delivered battle. The battle of Chancellorsville was fought--the most interesting battle of the war--in which the blended genius of Lee and Jackson illustrated to the world the highest achievement of generalship in the management of the lesser against the greatly superior force.

Again was the Army of the Potomac crushed and driven across the Rappahannock.

And now there arose a great question in the camp and in the council of State. It was a question of statesmanship as well as of arms. The question was answered by Lee withdrawing his army from before Hooker and proceeding through the lower Shenandoah Valley to Pennsylvania, leaving the road to Richmond open to be taken by the enemy if he should still prefer the policy of "on to Richmond." The motive of this movement was two-fold--to relieve Virginia of the enemy by forcing him to defend his own country, and by a possible great victory to affect public opinion of the North, and thus to conquer peace. The first object was accomplished; for as soon as Hooker discerned the movement of Lee, he hastened to follow and to put his army between Lee and Washington. Had Lee gained a crushing victory Baltimore and Washington would have been in his power, and then in all probability peace would have ensued. Public opinion in the North was greatly depressed, and sentiments of peace were ready to assert themselves. An incident illustrated this. As we were marching from Chambersburg to Gettysburg, I observed some ladies near the roadway wave their handkerchiefs to our passing troops. It excited my attention and curiosity. I rode up to them and said, "Ladies, I observed you waving your handkerchiefs as if in cheer to our army. Why so? We are your enemies and the enemies of your country." They replied: "We are tired of the war and want you to conquer peace." I was greatly impressed with their answer, and saw that there might be true patriotism in their act and hopes.

The invasion of Pennsylvania was wise and prudent from the standpoint of both arms and statesmanship. Everything promised success. Never was the Army of Northern Virginia in better condition. The troops had unbounded confidence in themselves and in their leaders. They were full of the fervor of patriotism--had abiding faith in their cause and in the favoring will of Heaven. There was an elation from the fact of invading the country of an enemy that had so cruelly invaded theirs. The spirit and elan of our soldiers was beyond description. They only could know it who felt it. They had the courage and dash to accomplish anything--everything but the impossible. On the contrary, the Federal army was never so dispirited, as I afterwards learned from some of its officers. And this was most natural. They marched from the bloody fields of Fredericksburg and Chancellorsville, the scenes of their humiliating and bloody defeat, to meet a foe from whom they had never won a victory.

But alas, how different the result! Gettysburg was such a sad ending to such high and well assured hopes! Things went untoward with our generals. And Providence itself, on which we had so much relied, seems to have led us by our mishaps to our own destruction.

The disastrous result of the campaign, in my opinion, was not due to the generalship of Lee, but wholly to the disregard of his directions by some of his generals. The chief among these, I regret to say, was the failure of General Stuart to follow the order*(*Lee's Report July 31, 1863, War Records, Series I, Vol. 27, Part 2, p. 300) of Lee, which directed him to move into Maryland, crossing the Potomac east or west of the Blue Ridge, as, in his judgment, should be best, and take position on the right of our column as it advanced. Instead of taking position on the right of our column as it advanced, Stuart followed the right of the Federal column, thus placing it between himself and Lee. The consequence was that Lee from the time he crossed the Potomac had no communication with Stuart until after the battle on the 1st of July, when he heard that Stuart was at Carlisle, and Stuart did not reach Gettysburg until the afternoon of July 2d. Lee, referring to Stuart, says: "By the route he pursued the Federal army war interposed between his command and our main body, preventing any communication with him until he arrived at Carlisle. The march toward Gettysburg was conducted more slowly than it would have been had the movements of the Federal army been known." * (*Id. p. 307.) These are solemn, mild words, but they cover the defeat at Gettysburg. Had Lee known the movements of the Federal army he could easily have had his whole army concentrated in Gettysburg on the 1st of July, and could easily have enveloped and crushed the enemy's advanced corps, and then defeated Meade in detail. But as it was, the encounter of the advance of the Federal army was a surprise to Lee.

Hill had on the 30th of June encamped with two of his divisions, Heth's and Pender's at Cashtown, about eight miles from Gettysburg. Next morning he moved with Heth's division, followed by Pender's toward Gettysburg. They encountered the enemy about three miles of the town. The enemy offered very determined resistance, but Heth's division, with great gallantry, drove him before it until it reached Seminary Heights, which overlooked Gettysburg. At this time, 2 P.M., Rodes' and Early's divisions of Ewell's corps--the first from Carlisle and the other from York, made their opportune appearance on the left of Heth and at right angles to it; then Pender's division was thrown forward, and all advancing together drove the enemy from position to position, and through the town, capturing 5,000 prisoners, and putting the enemy to flight in great disorder. Referring to this juncture of affairs, Col. Walter H. Taylor, in his "Four Years With Gen. Lee," says: "Genl. Lee witnessed the flight of the Federals through Gettysburg and up the hills beyond. He then directed me to go to Genl. Ewell and to say to him that from the position he occupied he could see the enemy retiring over the hills, without organization and in great confusion; that it was only necessary to press 'those people' in order to secure possession of the heights, and that, if possible, he wanted him to do this. In obedience to these instructions I proceeded immediately to Genl. Ewell and delivered the order of Genl. Lee." Genl. Ewell did not obey this order. Those heights were what is known as Cemetery Hill, which was the key to the Federal position. The enemy afterward, that night, with great diligence fortified those heights; and subsequently the lives of thousands of our soldiers were sacrificed in the vain effort to capture them. It was a fatal disobedience of orders. What if Jackson had been there? Col. Taylor would not have had any order to bear to him. Lee would have witnessed not only the fleeing enemy, but at the same time the hot pursuit of Stonewall Jackson. Ah! if Stuart had been there, to give one bugle blast and to set his squadrons on the charge! Alas! he was then twenty-five miles away at Carlisle, ignorant that a battle was on.

That afternoon after the fight was over, Anderson's division of Hill's corps arrived on the battle field and took position where Pender formerly was. At sunset Johnson's division of Ewell's corps came up and took line of battle on Early's left, and about midnight McLaws' division and Hood's division (except Laws' brigade) of Longstreet's corps encamped withing four miles of Gettysburg. The troops which had been engaged in the fight bivouacked on the positions won. I am thus particular to locate our troops in order to show who may be responsible for any errors of the next day.

Inasmuch as Meade's army was not fully up, it required no great generalship to determine that it would be to our advantage to make an attack as early in the next morning as possible. And it was no more than reasonable that every general having control of troops should feel and fully appreciate the imperious necessity of getting ready to do so and to be ready for prompt action.

General Lee determined to make the main attack on the enemy's left early in the morning. This attack was to be made by Longstreet, who was directed to take position on the right of Hill and on the Emmittsburg road. After a conference with the corps and division commanders the previous evening, it was understood that this attack was to be made as early as practicable by Longstreet, and he was to be supported by Anderson and to receive the co-operation of Ewell. General Fitzhugh Lee in his "Life of Lee," says: "When Lee went to sleep that night he was convinced that his dispositions for the battle next day were understood by the corps commanders, for he had imparted them to each in person. On the morning of July 2, Lee was up before light, breakfasted and was ready for the fray."

Can you believe it ? Can you even at this distant day altogether suppress a rising indignation-- that Longstreet did not get into line of battle until after 4 P. M., although he had the previous night encamped within four miles of Gettysburg? In the meanwhile Sickles had taken position in what is known as the Peach Orchard and on the Emmittsburg road, which were the positions assigned to Longstreet, and which he could have taken earlier in the day without firing a gun. The forces of the enemy had come up from long distances--Sedgwick had marched thirty-four miles since 9 P. M., of the day before and had gotten into line of battle before Longstreet did.

The attack was made. Sickles was driven from the Peach Orchard and the Emmittsburg road. Little Round Top and the Federal lines were penetrated, but they were so largely reinforced that the attack failed after the most courageous effort and great expenditure of lives. It has been stated that if this attack had been made in the morning as directed, Lee would have won a great victory, and the fighting of the 3d would have been saved. The attack on the left also failed. There, too, the lines and entrenchments of the enemy were penetrated, but they could not be held for want of simultaneous and conjoint action on the part of the commanders. Col. Taylor, speaking of this, says; "The whole affair was disjointed."

Thus ended the second day. General Lee determined to renew the attack on the morrow. He ordered Longstreet to make the attack next morning with his whole corps, and sent to aid him in the attack of Heth's division under Pettigrew, Lane's and Scales' brigades of Pender's division under General Trimble, and also Wilcox's brigade, and directed General Ewell to assail the enemy's right at the same time. "A careful examination," says Lee, "was made of the ground secured by Longstreet, and his batteries placed in position, which it was believed would enable them to silence those of the enemy. Hill's artillery and part of Ewell's was ordered to open simultaneously, and the assaulting column to advance under cover of the combined fire of the three. The batteries were directed to be pushed forward as the infantry progressed, protect their flanks and support their attacks closely." Every word of this order was potentially significant. You will thus observe Lee's plan of attack. It was to be made in the morning--presumably in the early morning--with the whole of Longstreet's corps, composed of the divisions of Pickett, McLaws and Hood, together with Heth's division, two brigades of Pender and Wilcox's brigade, and that the assaulting column was to advance under the cover of the combined fire of the artillery of the three corps, and that the assault was to be the combined assault of infantry and artillery-- the batteries to be pushed forward as the infantry progressed, to protect their flanks and support their attack closely. The attack was not made as here ordered. The attacking column did not move until 3 P. M., and when it did move it was without McLaws' and Hood's divisions and practically without Wilcox's brigade, and without accompanying artillery. The whole attacking force did not exceed 14,000, of which Pickett's division did not exceed 4,700. General Lee afterwards claimed that if the attack had been made as he ordered, it would have been successful.

In order to appreciate the charge made by the attacking force, it is necessary to have some idea of the relative strength and positions of the two armies, and of the topography of the country. Before the battle of Gettysburg opened on the 1st of July, Meade's army consisted of seven army corps which, with artillery and cavalry, numbered 105,000. Lee's army consisted of three army corps which, with artillery and cavalry, numbered 62,000. On the 3rd of July the enemy had six army corps in line of battle, with the Sixth corps held in reserve. Their right rested on Culp Hill and curved around westerly to Cemetery Hill, and thence extended southerly in a straight line along what is known as Cemetery Ridge to Round Top. This line was well protected along its whole length with either fortifications, stone walls or entrenchments. It was crowned with batteries, while the infantry was, in places, several ranks deep, with a line in the rear with skirmish lines in front. The form of the line was like a shepherd's crook. Our line extended from the enemy's right around to Seminary Ridge, which runs parallel to Cemetery Ridge, to a point opposite to Round Top. Between these two ridges lay an open, cultivated valley of about one mile wide, and through this valley ran the Emmittsburg road in a somewhat diagonal line, with a heavy fence on either side. The charge was to be made across this valley so as to strike the left centre of the enemy's line. The hope was that if we broke their right line, we would swing around to the left, rout and cut off their wing, where Stuart waited with his cavalry to charge upon them; and thus destroy or capture them, and put ourselves in possession of the Baltimore road and of a commanding position.

Such were the plans of the assault and such was the position of the hostile forces. Lee's plan to make an assault was dangerous and hazardous, but he was pressed by the force of circumstances which we cannot now consider. The success of his plan depended largely on the promptness and co-operation of his generals. Without this there could be little hope of success. He gave his orders and retired for to-morrow.

All wait on the to-morrow. And now the 3d of July has come. The summer sun early heralded by roseate dawn, rises serenely and brightly from beyond the wooded hills. No darkening clouds obscure his bright and onward way. His aspect is as joyous as when Eden first bloomed under his rays. Earth and heaven are in happy accord. The song of birds, the chirp and motion of winged insects greet the early morn. The wild flowers and the cultivated grain of the fields are glad in their beauty and fruitage. The streams joyously ripple on their accustomed way, and the trees lift and wave their leafy branches in the warm, life-giving air. Never was sky or earth more serene-- more harmonious--more aglow with light and life.

In blurring discord with it all was man alone. Thousands and tens of thousands of men-- once happy fellow countrymen, now in arms, had gathered in hostile hosts and in hostile confronting lines. It was not the roseate dawn nor rising sun that awoke them from the sleep of wearied limbs. Before the watching stars had withdrawn from their sentinel posts, the long roll, the prelude of battle, had sounded their reveille, and rudely awoke them from fond dreams of home and loved ones far away. For two days had battle raged. On the first, when the field was open and equal, the soldiers of the South, after most determined resistance, had driven their foe before them from position to position--from valley to hill top, through field and through the town, to the heights beyond. On the second day, on our right and on our left, with heroic valor and costly blood, they had penetrated the lines and fortifications of the enemy, but were too weak to hold the prize of positions gained against overpowering numbers of concentrated reinforcements. The dead and wounded marked the lines of the fierce combat. The exploded caissons, the dismounted cannon, the dead artillery horses, the scattered rifles, the earth soaked with human gore--the contorted forms of wounded men, and the white, cold faces of the dead, made a mockery and sad contrast to the serene and smiling face of the skies.

From the teamsters to the general in chief it was known that the battle was yet undecided --that the fierce combat was to be renewed. All knew that victory won or defeat suffered, was to be at a fearful cost--that the best blood of the land was to flow copiously as a priceless oblation to the god of battle. The intelligent soldiers of the South knew and profoundly felt that the hours were potential--that on them possibly hung the success of their cause--the peace and independence of the Confederacy. They knew that victory meant so much more to them than to the enemy. It meant to us uninvaded and peaceful homes under our own rule and under our own nationality. With us it was only to be let alone. With this end in view, all felt that victory was to be won at any cost. All were willing to die, if only their country could thereby triumph. And fatal defeat meant much to the enemy. It meant divided empire--lost territory and severed population. Both sides felt that the hours were big with the fate of empire. The sense of the importance of the issue, and the responsibility of fully doing duty equal to the grand occasion, impressed on us all a deep solemnity and a seriousness of thought that left no play for gay moods or for sympathy with nature's smiling aspect, however gracious. Nor did we lightly consider the perils of our duty. From our position in line of battle, which we had taken early in the morning, we could see the frowning and cannon-crowned heights far off held by the enemy. In a group of officers, a number of whom did not survive that fatal day, I could not help expressing that it was to be another Malvern Hill, another costly day to Virginia and to Virginians. While all fully saw and appreciated the cost and the fearful magnitude of the assault, yet all were firmly resolved, if possible, to pluck victory from the very jaws of death itself. Never were men more conscious of the difficulty imposed on them by duty, or more determinedly resolved to perform it with alacrity and cheerfulness, even to annihilation, than were the men of Pickett's division on that day. With undisturbed fortitude and even with ardent impatience did they await the command for the assault. The quiet of the day had been unbroken save on our extreme left, where in the early morning there had been some severe fighting; but this was soon over, and now all on both sides were at rest, waiting in full expectancy of the great assault, which the enemy, as well as we, knew was to be delivered. The hours commenced to go wearily by. The tension on our troops had become great. The midday sun had reached the zenith, and poured its equal and impartial rays between the opposite ridges that bounded the intervening valley running North and South. Yet no sound or stir broke the ominous silence. Both armies were waiting spectators for the great event. Upwards of one hundred thousand unengaged soldiers were waiting as from a grand amphitheatre to witness the most magnificent heroic endeavor in arms that ever immortalized man. Still the hours lingered on. Why the delay? There is a serious difference of opinion between the general in chief and his most trusted lieutenant general as to the wisdom of making the assault. Lee felt, from various considerations, the forced necessity of fighting out the battle here, and having the utmost confidence in his troops he fully expected victory if the attack be made as he had ordered. Longstreet, foreseeing the great loss of assaulting the entrenched position of the enemy and making such assault over such a distance under the concentrated fire, urges that the army should be moved beyond the enemy's left flank, with the hope of forcing him thus to abandon his stronghold or to fight us to our advantage. Longstreet pressed this view and delayed giving the necessary orders until Lee more pre-emptorily repeated his own order to make the assault. Even then Longstreet was so reluctant to carry out the orders of Lee that he placed upon Lt-Col. Alexander, who was in charge of the artillery on this day, the responsibility of virtually giving the order for its execution.

At last, in our immediate front, at 1 P. M., there suddenly leaped from one of our cannons a single sharp, far-reaching sound, breaking the long-continued silence and echoing along the extended lines of battle and far beyond the far-off heights. All were now at a strained attention. Then quickly followed another gun. Friend and foe at once recognized that these were signal guns. Then hundreds of cannon opened upon each other from the confronting heights. What a roar--how incessant! The earth trembled under the mighty resound of cannon. The air is darkened with sulphurous clouds. The whole valley is enveloped. The sun, lately so glaring, is itself obscured. Nothing can be seen but the flashing light leaping from the cannon's mouth amidst the surrounding smoke. The air which was so silent and serene is now full of exploding and screaming shells and shot, as if the earth had opened and let out the very furies of Avernus. The hurtling and death-dealing missiles are plowing amidst batteries, artillery and lines of infantry, crushing, mangling and killing until the groans of the men mingle with the tempest's sound. The storm of battle rages. It is appalling, terrific, yet grandly exciting. It recalls the imagery of Byron's night-storm amidst the Alps:

"The sky is changed, and such a change!* * *

* * * * * * * * * * * Far along

From peak to peak, the rattling crags among

Leaps the live thunder! Not from one lone cloud,

But every mountain now hath found a tongue,

And Jura answers from her misty shroud

Back to the joyous Alps who call to her aloud."

After two hours of incessant firing the storm at last subsides. It has been a grand and fit prelude to what is now to follow. All is again silent. Well knowing what is shortly to follow, all watch in strained expectancy. The waiting is short. Only time for Pickett to report to his lieutenant-general his readiness and to receive the word of command. Pickett said: "General, shall I advance?" Longstreet turned away his face and did not speak. Pickett repeated the question. Longstreet, without opening his lips, bowed in answer. Pickett, in a determined voice, said: "Sir, I shall lead my division forward," and galloped back and gave the order, "Forward march!" The order ran down through brigade, regimental and company officers to the men. The men with alacrity and cheerfulness fell into line. Kemper's brigade on the right, Garnett's on his left, with Heth's division on the left of Garnett, formed the first line. Armistead's brigade moved in rear of Garnett's, and Lane's and Scales' brigades of Pender's division moved in rear of Heth, but not in touch nor in line with Armistead. As the lines cleared the woods that skirted the brow of the ridge and passed through our batteries, with their flags proudly held aloft, waving in the air, with polished muskets and swords gleaming and flashing in the sunlight, they presented an inexpressibly grand and inspiring sight. It is said that when our troops were first seen there ran along the line of the Federals, as from men who had waited long in expectancy, the cry: There they come! There they come! The first impression made by the magnificent array of our lines as they moved forward, was to inspire the involuntary admiration of the enemy. Then they realized that they came, terrible as an army with banners. Our men moved with quick step as calmly and orderly as if they were on parade. No sooner than our lines came in full view, the enemy's batteries in front, on the right and on the left, from Cemetery Hill to Round Top, opened on them with a concentrated, accurate and fearful fire of shell and solid shot. These plowed through or exploded in our ranks, making great havoc. Yet they made no disturbance. As to the orderly conduct and steady march of our men, they were as if they had not been. As the killed and wounded dropped out, our lines closed and dressed up, as if nothing had happened, and went on with steady march. I remember I saw a shell explode amidst the ranks of the left company of the regiment on our right. Men fell like ten-pins in a ten-strike. Without a pause and without losing step, the survivors dressed themselves to their line and our regiment to the diminished regiment, and all went on as serenely and as unfalteringly as before. My God! it was magnificent--this march of our men. What was the inspiration that gave them this stout courage--this gallant bearing--this fearlessness--this steadiness--this collective and individual heroism? It was home and country. It was the fervor of patriotism--the high sense of individual duty. It was blood and pride of state--the inherited quality of a brave and honorable ancestry.

On they go--down the sloping sides of the ridge--across the valley--over the double fences--up the slope that rises to the heights crowned with stone walls and entrenchments, studded with batteries, and defended by multiple lines of protected infantry. The skirmish line is driven in. And now there bursts upon our ranks in front and on flank, like sheeted hail, a new storm of missiles--cannister, shrapnel and rifle shot. Still the column advances steadily and onward, without pause or confusion. Well might Count de Paris describe it as an irresistible machine moving forward which nothing could stop. The dead and wounded officers and men-- mark each step of advance. Yet under the pitiless rain of missiles the brave men move on, and then with a rush and cheering yell they reach the stone wall. Our flags are planted on the defenses. Victory seems within grasp, but more is to be done. Brave Armistead, coming up, overleaps the wall and calls on all to follow. Brave men follow his lead. Armistead is now among the abandoned cannon, making ready to turn them against their former friends. Our men are widening the breach of the penetrated and broken lines of the Federals. But, now the enemy has made a stand, and are rallying. It is a critical moment. That side must win which can command instant reinforcements. They come not to Armistead, but they come to Webb, and they come to him from every side in overwhelming numbers in our front and with enclosing lines on either flank. They are pushed forward. Armistead is shot down with mortal wounds and heavy slaughter is made of those around him. The final moment has come when there must be instant flight, instant surrender, or instant death. Each alternative is shared. Less than 1,000 escape of all that noble division which in the morning numbered 4,700; all the rest either killed, wounded or captured. All is over. As far as possible for mortals they approached the accomplishment of the impossible. Their great feat of arms has closed. The charge of Pickett's division has been proudly, gallantly and right royally delivered.

And then, at once, before our dead are counted, there arose from that bloody immortalized field, Fame, the Mystic Goddess, and from her trumpet in clarion notes there rang out upon the ear of the world the story of Pickett's charge at Gettysburg. All over this country, equally North and South, millions listened and returned applause. Over ocean Fame wings her way. Along the crowded population and cities of Europe she rings out the story. The people of every brave race intently listen and are thrilled. Over the famous battlefields of modern and ancient times she sweeps. Over the ruins and dust of Rome the story is heralded. Thermopylae bears and applauds. The ancient pyramids catch the sound, and summing up the records of their hoary centuries, searching, find therein no story of equal courage. Away over the mounds of buried cities Fame challenges, in vain, a response from their past. Over the continents and the isles of the sea the story runs. The whole world is tumultuous with applause. A new generation has heard the story with undiminished admiration and praise. It is making its way up through the opening years to the opening centuries. The posterities of all the living will gladly hear and treasure it, and will hand it down to the end of time as an inspiration and example of courage to all who shall hereafter take up arms.

The intrinsic merit of the charge of Pickett's men at Gettysburg, is too great, too broad, too immortal for the limitations of sections, of states, or of local pride.

The people of this great and growing republic, now so happily reunited, have and feel a common kinship and a common heritage in this peerless example of American courage and American heroism.

But let us return to the battlefield to view our dead, our dying and our wounded. Here they lie scattered over the line of their march; here at the stone wall they lie in solid heaps along its foot; and here within the Federal lines they are as autumnal leaves--each and all precious heroes--each the loved one of some home in dear, dear Virginia. Now we seem to catch the sound of another strain. It is more human; it touches pathetically more closely human hearts. It is the wailing voice of afflicted love. It is the sobbing outburst of the sorrow of bereavement coming up from so many homes and families, from so many kinsmen and friends; and with it comes the mournful lamentations of Virginia herself, the mother of us all, over the loss of so many of her bravest and best sons.

Of her generals Garnett is dead, Armistead is dying; and Kemper desperately wounded. Of her colonels of regiments six are killed on the field, Hodges, Edmonds, Magruder, Williams, Patton, Allen, and Owen is dying and Stuart mortally wounded. Three lieutenant-colonels are killed, Calcutt, Wade and Ellis. Five colonels, Hunton, Terry, Garnett, Mayo and Aylett, are wounded. Four lieutenant-colonels commanding regiments, Martin, Carrington, Otey and Richardson are wounded. Of the whole compliment of field officers in fifteen regiments only one escaped unhurt, Lieutenant-Colonel Joseph C. Cabell. The loss of company officers are in equal proportion. It is a sad, mournful summing up. Let the curtain fall on the tragic scene.

But there are some of those who fell on that field whom I cannot pass by with a mere enumeration.

Gen. Lewis A. Armistead, the commander of our brigade, is one of these. Fortune made him the most advanced and conspicuous hero of that great charge. He was to us the very embodiment of a heroic commander. On this memorable day be placed himself on foot in front of his brigade. He drew his sword, placed his hat on its point, proudly held it up as a standard, and strode in front of his men, calm, self-collected, resolute and fearless. All he asked was that his men should follow him. Thus in front he marched until within about one hundred paces of the stone wall some officer on horseback, whose name I have never been able to learn, stopped him for some purpose. The few moments of detention thus caused were sufficient to put him for the first time in the rear of his advancing brigade. Then quickly on he came, and when he reached the stone wall where others stopped, he did not pause an instant--over it he went and called on all to follow. He fell, as above stated, amidst the enemy's guns, mortally wounded. He was taken to the Eleventh Corps' Hospital, and in a few days he died and was buried there.

Another: Col. James Gregory Hodges, of the 14th Virginia, of Armistead's brigade, fell instantly killed at the foot of the stone wall of the Bloody Angle, and around and over his dead body there was literally a pile of his dead officers around him, including gallant Major Poor. On the occasion of the reunion of Pickett's Division at Gettysburg, 1887, General Hunt, chief of the Federal artillery at this battle, who had known Col. Hodges before the war, pointed out to me where he saw him lying dead among his comrades. He led his regiment in this memorable charge with conspicuous courage and gallantry. He was an able and experienced officer. At the breaking out of the war he was Colonel of the Third Virginia Volunteers, and from 20th April, 1861, until he fell at Gettysburg he served with distinguished ability, zeal and gallantry his State and the Confederacy. He was with his regiment in every battle in which it was engaged in the war. He commanded the love and confidence of his men, and they cheerfully and fearlessly ever followed his lead. His memory deserves to be cherished and held in the highest esteem by his city, to which by his virtues, character and patriotic service he brought honor and consideration.

Col. John C. Owens, of the Ninth Virginia, Armistead's Brigade, also of this city, fell mortally wounded on the charge, and died in the field hospital that night. He had been recently promoted to the colonelcy of the regiment from the captaincy of the Portsmouth Rifles, Company G. As adjutant of the regiment I had every opportunity of knowing and appreciating Col. Owens as a man and officer. I learned to esteem and love him. He was intelligent, quiet, gentle, kind and considerate. Yet he was firm of purpose and of strong will. He knew how to command and how to require obedience. He was faithful, and nothing could swerve him from duty. Under his quiet, gentle manner there was a force of character surprising to those who did not know him well. And he was as brave and heroic as he was gentle and kind. Under fire he was cool, self-possessed, and without fear. He was greatly beloved and respected by his regiment, although he had commanded it for a very short time. He fell while gallantly leading his regiment before it reached the enemy's lines. He, too, is to be numbered among those heroes of our city, who left home, never to return; who after faithful and distinguished service, fell on the field of honor, worthy of the high rank he had attained, reflecting by his life, patriotism and courage, honor on his native city, which will never let his name and patriotic devotion be forgotten.

John C. Niemeyer, First Lieutenant I, Ninth Virginia, was killed in that charge just before reaching the famous stone wall. He was a born soldier, apt, brave, dashing. He was so young, so exuberant in feeling, so joyous in disposition, that in my recollection of him he seems to have been just a lad. Yet he knew and felt the responsibility of office, and faithfully and gallantly discharged its duties. He was a worthy brother of the distinguished Col. W. F. Neimeyer, a brilliant officer who also gave his young life to the cause,

And there, too, fell my intimate friend, John S. Jenkins, Adjutant of the Fourteenth Virginia. He, doubtless, was one of those gallant officers whom General Hunt saw when he recognized Colonel Hodges immediately after the battle, lying dead where he fell, who had gathered around him, and whose limbs were interlocked in death as their lives had been united in friendship and comradeship in the camp. He fell among the bravest, sealed his devotion to his country by his warm young blood, in the flush of early vigorous manhood when his life was full of hope and promise. He gave up home which was secularly dear and sweet to him, when he knew that hereafter his only home would be under the flag of his regiment, wherever it might lead, whether on the march, in the camp or on the battle field. His life was beautiful and manly--his death was heroic and glorious, and his name is of the imperishable ones of Pickett's charge.

Time fails me to do more than mention among those from our city who were killed at Gettysburg: Lieut. Robert Guy, Lieut. George W. Mitchell, John A. F. Dunderdale, Lemuel H. Williams, W. B. Bennett, John W. Lattimore, W. G. Monte, Richard J. Nash, Thomas C. Owens, Daniel Byrd, John Cross and Joshua Murden--heroes all--who contributed to the renown of Pickett's charge, gave new lustre to the prowess of arms, and laid a new chaplet of glory on the brow of Virginia, brighter and more immortal than all others worn by her.

"Let marble shafts and sculptured urns

Their names record, their actions tell,

Let future ages read and learn

How well they fought, how nobly fell."

(Source: Southern Historical Society Papers, Vol. 33, pages 118-134)

[From the Times-Dispatch, April 10, 1904.]

THE BATTLE OF GETTYSBURG

––––––––––

And the Charge of Pickett's Division.

––––––––––

ACCOUNTS OF COLONEL RAWLEY MARTIN AND CAPTAIN

JOHN HOLMES SMITH.

––––––––––

With Prefatory Note by U. S. Senator John W. Daniel.

––––––––––

[Very much has been published regarding the momentous battle of Gettysburg, but the following additions can but be welcome to our readers. Reference may be made to ante p. 33 and preceding volumes of the Southern Historical Society Papers, particularly the early volumes, II-X inclusive.--Editor.]

Washington, D. C., March 30, 1904

Editor of The Times-Dispatch:

Sir,--Enclosed are accounts of the charge at Gettysburg by two officers of Pickett's Division of high reputation for courage an reliability--the one being Lieutenant-Colonel Rawley W. Martin, then of the 53d Virginia Infantry, Armistead's Brigade, and the other Captain John Holmes Smith, of the Lynchburg Home Guard, who, after Lieutenant-Colonel Kirkwood Otey, and Major Risque Hutter, were wounded in that battle, commanded the 11th Virginia Infantry.

In 1897 Commander Sylvester Chamberlain, of an Association of United States Naval Veterans, of Buffalo, New York, wrote to Colonel Martin (now Dr. Martin, of Lynchburg, Va.), asking him to recount the charge, saying:

"The charge of Pickett's Division outrivals the storied heroism of the Old Guard of Napoleon. They knew no such battle as that of Gettysburg, and, I believe, the old First Confederate Army Corps could have whipped the best two corps in Napoleon's army, taken in the zenith of his fame."

Dr. Martin wrote this paper under the call from a Northern camp commander.

Captain John Holmes Smith was with his regiment on the right wing of Pickett's charge, under Kemper, and struck the Federal line to the right of where General Armistead made the break. The soldiers of Kemper there took the Federal entrenchments, and remained about twenty minutes in possession of them. Twice couriers were sent back for reinforcements. Slowly, but surely, the details of this magnificent exploit of war come to light; and the more brilliant does it appear. Slowly, and surely, also do the evidences gather that point toward the responsible agents of the failure that ensued.

Respectfully,

Jno. W. Daniel.

COLONEL RAWLEY MARTIN'S ACCOUNT.

Lynchburg Va., August 11, 1897.

Commander Sylvester Chamberlain, Buffalo, N. Y.:

My dear Sir,--In the effort to comply with your request to describe Pickett's charge at Gettysburg, I may unavoidably repeat what has often been told before, as the position of troops, the cannonade, the advance, and the final disaster are familiar to all who have the interest or the curiosity to read. My story will be short, for I shall only attempt to describe what fell under my own observation.

You ask for a description of the "feelings of the brave Virginians who passed through that hell of fire in their heroic charge on Cemetery Ridge." The esprit du corps could not have been better; the men were in good physical condition, self reliant and determined. They felt the gravity of the situation, for they knew well the metal of the foe in their front; they were serious and resolute, but not disheartened. None of the usual jokes, common on the eve of battle, were indulged in, for every man felt his individual responsibility, and realized that he had the most stupendous work of his life before him; officers and men knew at what cost and at what risk the advance was to be made, but they had deliberately made up their minds to attempt it. I believe the general sentiment of the division was that they would succeed in driving the Federal line from what was their objective point; they knew that many, very many, would go down under the storm of shot and shell which would greet them when their gray ranks were spread out to view, but it never occurred to them that disaster would come after they once placed their tattered banners upon the crest of Seminary Ridge.

THEIR NERVE.

I believe if those men had been told: "This day your lives will pay the penalty of your attack upon the Federal lines," they would have made the charge just as it was made. There was no straggling, no feigned sickness, no pretense of being overcome by the intense heat; every man felt that it was his duty to make that fight; that he was his own commander, and they would have made the charge without an officer of any description; they only needed to be told what they were expected to do. This is as near the feeling of the men of Pickett's Division on the morning of the battle as I can give, and with this feeling they went to their work. Many of them were veteran soldiers, who had followed the little cross of stars from Big Bethel to Gettysburg; they knew their own power, and they knew the temper of their adversary; they had often met before, and they knew the meeting before them would be desperate and deadly.

THE ALIGNMENT.

Pickett's three little Virginia brigades were drawn up in two lines, Kemper on the right (1st, 3d, 7th, 11th and 24), Garnett on the left (8th, 18th, 19th, 28th and 56th), and Armistead in the rear and center (9th, 14th, 38th, 53d and 57th) Virginia Regiments, covering the space between Kemper's left and Garnett's right flanks. This position was assigned Armistead, I suppose, that he might at the critical moment rush to the assistance of the two leading brigades, and if possible, put the capstone upon their work. We will see presently how he succeeded. The Confederate artillery was on the crest of Seminary Ridge, nearly in front of Pickett; only a part of the division had the friendly shelter of the woods; the rest endured the scorching rays of the July sun until the opening of the cannonade, when the dangers from the Federal batteries were added to their discomfort. About 1 o'clock two signal guns were fired by the Washington Artillery, and instantly a terrific cannonade was commenced, which lasted for more than an hour, when suddenly everything was silent. Every man knew what that silence portended. The grim blue battle line on Seminary Ridge began at once to prepare for the advance of its antagonists; both sides felt that the tug of war was about to come, and that Greek must meet Greek as they had never met before.

A SOLEMN MOMENT.

From this point, I shall confine my description to events connected with Armistead's brigade, with which I served. Soon after the cannonade ceased, a courier dashed up to General Armistead, who was pacing up and down in front of the 53d Virginia Regiment, his battalion of direction (which I commanded in the charge and at the head of which Armistead marched), and gave him the order from General Pickett to prepare for the advance. At once the command "Attention, battalion!" rang out clear and distinct. Instantly every man was on his feet and in his place; the alignment was made with as much coolness and precision as if preparing for dress parade. Then Armistead went up to the color sergeant of the 53d Virginia Regiment and said: "Sergeant, are you going to put those colors on the enemy's works to-day?" The gallant fellow replied: "I will try, sir, and if mortal man can do it, it shall be done." It was done, but not until this brave man, and many others like him, had fallen with their faces to the foe; bur never once did that banner trail in the dust, for some brave fellow invariably caught it as it was going down, and again bore it aloft, until Armistead saw its tattered folds unfurled on the very crest of Seminary Ridge.

THE ADVANCE.

After this exchange of confidence between the general and the color-bearer, Armistead commanded: "Right shoulder, shift arms. Forward, march." They stepped out at quick time, in perfect order and alignment--tramp, tramp, up to the Emmittsburg road; then the advancing Confederates saw the long line of blue, nearly a mile distant, ready and awaiting their coming. The scene was grand and terrible, and well calculated to demoralize the stoutest heart; but not a step faltered, not an elbow lost the touch of its neighbor, not a face blanched, for these men had determined to do their whole duty, and reckoned not the cost. On they go; at about 1,100 yards the Federal batteries opened fire; the advancing Confederates encounter and sweep before them the Federal skirmish line. Still forward they go; hissing, screaming shells break in their front, rear, on their flanks, all about them, but the devoted band, with the blue line in their front as their objective point, press forward, keeping step to the music of the battle. The distance between the opposing forces grows less and less, until suddenly the infantry behind the rock fence poured volley after volley into the advancing ranks. The men fell like stalks of grain before the reaper, but still they closed the gaps and pressed forward through that pitiless storm. The two advance brigades have thus far done the fighting. Armistead has endured the terrible ordeal without firing a gun; his brave followers have not changed their guns from the right shoulder. Great gaps have been torn in their ranks; their field and company officers have fallen; color-bearer after color-bearer has been shot down, but still they never faltered.

THE CRITICAL MOMENT.

At the critical moment, in response to a request from Kemper, Armistead, bracing himself to the desperate blow, rushed forward to Kemper's and Garnett's line, delivered his fire, and with one supreme effort planted his colors on the famous rock fence. Armistead himself, with his hat on the point of his sword, that his men might see it through the smoke of battle, rushed forward, scaled the wall, and cried: "Boys, give them the cold steel!" By this time, the Federal hosts lapped around both flanks and made a counter advance in their front, and the remnant of those three little brigades melted away. Armistead himself had fallen, mortally wounded, under the guns he had captured, while the few who followed him over the fence were either dead or wounded. The charge was over, the sacrifice had been made, but, in the words of a Federal officer: "Banks of heroes they were; they fled not, but amidst that still continuous and terrible fire they slowly, sullenly recrossed the plain--all that was left of them--but few of the five thousand."

WHERE WAS PICKETT.

When the advance commenced General Pickett rode up and down in rear of Kemper and Garnett, and in this position he continued as long as there was opportunity of observing him. When the assault became so fierce that he had to superintend the whole line, I am sure he was in his proper place. A few years ago Pickett's staff held a meeting in the city of Richmond, Va., and after comparing recollections, they published a statement to the effect that he was with the division throughout the charge; that he made an effort to secure reinforcements when he saw his flanks were being turned, and one of General Garnett's couriers testified that he carried orders from him almost to the rock fence. From my knowledge of General Pickett I am sure he was where his duty called him throughout the engagement. He was too fine a soldier, and had fought too many battles not to be where he was most needed on that supreme occasion of his military life.

The ground over which the charge was made was an open terrene, with slight depressions and elevations, but insufficient to be serviceable to the advancing column. At the Emmettsburg road, where the parallel fences impeded the onward march, large numbers were shot down on account of the crowding at the openings where the fences had been thrown down, and on account of the halt in order to climb the fences. After passing these obstacles, the advancing column deliberately rearranged its lines and moved forward. Great gaps were made in their ranks as they moved on, but they were closed up as deliberately and promptly as if on the parade ground; the touch of elbows was always to the centre, the men keeping constantly in view the little emblem which was their beacon light to guide them to glory and to death.

INSTANCES OF COURAGE.

I will mention a few instances of individual coolness and bravery exhibited in the charge. In the 53d Virginia Regiment, I saw every man of Company F (Captain Henry Edmunds, now a distinguished member of the Virginia bar) thrown flat to the earth by the explosion of a shell from Round Top, but every man who was not killed or desperately wounded sprang to his feet, collected himself and moved forward to close the gap made in the regimental front. A soldier from the same regiment was shot on the shin; he stopped in the midst of that terrific fire, rolled up his trousers leg, examined his wound, and went forward even to the rock fence. He escaped further injury, and was one of the few who returned to his friends, but so bad was his wound that it was nearly a year before he was fit for duty. When Kemper was riding off, after asking Armistead to move up to his support, Armistead called him, and, pointing to his brigade, said: "Did you ever see a more perfect line than that on dress parade?" It was, indeed, a lance head of steel, whose metal had been tempered in the furnace of conflict. As they were about to enter upon their work, Armistead, as was invariably his custom on going into battle, said: "Men, remember your wives, your mothers, your sisters and you sweethearts." Such an appeal would have made those men assault the ramparts of the infernal regions.

AFTER THE CHARGE.

You asked me to tell how the field looked after the charge, and how the men went back. This I am unable to do, as I was disabled at Armistead's side a moment after he had fallen, and left on the Federal side of the stone fence. I was picked up by the Union forces after their lines were reformed, and I take this occasion to express my grateful recollection of the attention I received on the field, particularly from Colonel Hess, of the 72d Pennsylvania (I think). If he still lives, I hope yet to have the pleasure of grasping his hand and expressing to him my gratitude for his kindness to me. Only the brave know how to treat a fallen foe.

I cannot close this letter without reference to the Confederate chief, General R. E. Lee. Somebody blundered at Gettysburg but not Lee. He was too great a master of the art of war to have hurled a handful of men against an army. It has been abundantly shown that the fault lay not with him, but with others, who failed to execute his orders.

This has been written amid interruptions, and is an imperfect attempt to describe the great charge, but I have made the effort to comply with your request because of your very kind and friendly letter, and because there is no reason why those who once were foes should not now be friends. The quarrel was not personal, but sectional, and although we tried to destroy each other thirty-odd years ago, there is no reason why we should cherish resentment against each other now.

I should be very glad to meet you in Lynchburg if your business or pleasure should ever bring you to Virginia.

With great respect,

Yours most truly,

Rawley W. Martin.

———————

CAPTAIN JOHN HOLMES SMITH'S ACCOUNT.

Lynchburg, Va., Feb. 4th and 5th.

John Holmes Smith, formerly Captain of Company G (the Home Guard), of Lynchburg, Va., and part of the 11th Virginia Infantry, Kemper's Brigade, Pickett's Division, 1st Corps (Longstreet), C. S. A., commanded that company, and then the regiment for a time in the battle of Gettysburg. He says as follows, concerning that battle:

The 11th Virginia Infantry arrived near Gettysburg, marching from Chambersburg on the afternoon of July 2d, 1863. We halted in sight of shells bursting in the front.

Very early on the morning of the 3d July we formed in rear of the Confederate artillery near Spurgeon's woods, where we lay for many hours. I noticed on the early morning as we were taking positions the long shadows cast by the figures of the men, their legs appearing to lengthen immediately as the shadows fell.

The 11th Virginia was the right regiment of Kemper's Brigade and of Pickett's Division. No notable event occurred in the morning, nor was there any firing of note near us that specially attracted my attention.

SIGNAL GUNS.

About 1 o'clock there was the fire of signal guns, and there were outbursts of artillery on both sides. Our artillery on the immediate front of the regiment was on the crest of the ridge, and our infantry line was from one to 250 yards in rear of it.

We suffered considerable loss before we moved. I had twenty-nine men in my company for duty that morning. Edward Valentine and two Jennings brothers (William Jennings) of my company were killed; De Witt Guy, sergeant, was wounded, and some of the men--a man now and a man then--were also struck and sent to the rear before we moved forward--I think about ten killed and wounded in that position. Company E, on my right, lost more seriously than Company G, and was larger in number.

LONGSTREET'S PRESENCE.

Just before the artillery fire ceased General Longstreet rode in a walk between the artillery and the infantry, in front of the regiment toward the left and disappeared down the line. He was as quiet as an old farmer riding over his plantation on a Sunday morning, and looked neither to the right or left.

It had been known for hours that we were to assail the enemy's lines in front. We fully expected to take them.

Presently the artillery ceased firing. Attention ! was the command. Our skirmishers were thrown to the front, and "forward, quick time, march," was the word given. We were ordered not to fire until so commanded. Lieutenant-Colonel Kirkwood Otey was thus in command of the regiment when we passed over the crest of the ridge, through our guns there planted, and had advanced some distance down the slope in our front. I was surprised before that our skirmishers had been brought to a stand by those of the enemy; and the latter only gave ground when our line of battle had closed up well inside of a hundred yards of our own skirmishers. The enemy's skirmishers then retreated in perfect order, firing as they fell back.

The enemy's artillery, front and flank, fired upon us, and many of the regiment were struck.

UP THE HILL.

Having descended the slope and commenced to ascend the opposite slope that rises toward the enemy's works, the Federal skirmishers kept up their fire until we were some four hundred yards from the works. They thus being between two fires--for infantry fire broke out from the works-- threw down their arms, rushed into our lines, and then sought refuge in the depression, waterway or gully between the slopes.

There was no distinct change of front; but "close and dress to the left" was the command, and this gave us an oblique movement to the left as we pressed ranks in that direction.

Our colors were knocked down several times as we descended the slope on our side. Twice I saw the color-bearer stagger and the next man seize the staff and go ahead; the third time the colors struck the ground as we were still on the down slope. The artillery had opened upon us with canister. H. V. Harris, adjutant of the regiment, rushed to them and seized them, and, I think, carried them to the enemy's works.

AT THE WORKS.

When the enemy's infantry opened fire on us--and we were several hundred yards distant from them as yet--we rushed towards the works, running, I may say, almost at top speed, and as we neared the works I could see a good line of battle, thick and substantial, firing upon us. When inside of a hundred yards of them I could see, first, a few, and then more and more, and presently, to my surprise and disgust, the whole line break away in flight. When we got to the works, which were a hasty trench and embankment, and not a stone wall at the point we struck, our regiment was a mass or ball, all mixed together, without company organization. Some of the 24th and 3d seemed to be coming with us, and it may be others. Not a man could I see in the enemy's works, but on account of the small timber and the lay of the ground, I could not see very far along the line, either right or left, of the position we occupied.

There were, as I thought at the time I viewed the situation, about three hundred men in the party with me, or maybe less. Adjutant H. V. Harris, of the regimental staff, was there dismounted. Captain Fry, Assistant Adjutant-General of General Kemper, was also there on foot, with a courier, who was a long-legged, big-footed fellow, whom we called "Big Foot Walker," also afoot. Captain R. W. Douthat, of Company F, I also noticed, and there were some other regimental officers whom I cannot now recall.

BIG FOOT WALKER.

We thought our work was done, and that the day was over, for the last enemy in sight we had seen disappear over the hill in front; and I expected to see General Lee's army marching up to take possession of the field. As I looked over the work of our advance with this expectation, I could see nothing but dead and wounded men and horses in the field beyond us, and my heart never in my life sank as it did then. It was a grievous disappointment.

Instantly men turned to each other with anxious inquiries what to do, and a number of officers grouped together in consultation, Captain Fry, Captain Douthat, Adjutant Harris, and myself, who are above noted, amongst them. No field officer appeared at this point that I could discover. We promptly decided to send a courier for reinforcements. No mounted man was there. "Big Foot Walker" was dispatched on that errand. Fearing some mishap to him, for shots from the artillery on our right, from the enemy's left, were still sweeping the field, we in a few moments sent another courier for reinforcements.

We were so anxious to maintain the position we had gained, that we watched the two men we had sent to our rear across the field, and saw them both, the one after the other, disappear over the ridge from which we had marched forward.

WAIT FOR TWENTY MINUTES.

Unmolested from the front or on either side, and with nothing to indicate that we would be assailed, we thus remained for fully twenty minutes after Walker had been sent for reinforcements--waited long after he had disappeared on his mission over the ridge in our rear.

Seeing no sign of coming help, anticipating that we would soon be attacked, and being in no condition of numbers or power to resist any serious assault, we soon concluded--that is, the officers above referred to--to send the men back to our lines, and we so ordered.

Lest they might attract the fire of the guns that still kept up a cannonade from the enemy's left, we told the men to scatter as they retired, and they did fall back singly and in small groups, the officers before named retiring also. Only Captain Ro. W. Douthat and myself remained at the works, while the rest of the party we were with, retired. I remained to dress a wound on my right leg, which was bleeding freely, and Douthat, I suppose, just to be with me. I dropped to the ground under the shade of the timber after the men left, pulled out a towel from my haversack, cut it into strips, and bandaged my thigh, through which a bullet had passed.

This wound had been received as we approached the enemy's skirmishers on the descending slope, one of them having shot me. I thought at the time I was knocked out, but did not fall, and I said to James R. Kent, sergeant: "Take charge of the company, I am shot." But soon finding I could move my leg and that I could go on, no bones being broken, I went to the end of the charge.

GETTING AWAY.

While I was still bandaging my leg at the works, my companion, Captain Robert W. Douthat, who had picked up a musket, commenced firing and fired several shots. Thinking he had spied an enemy in the distance, I continued bandaging my leg, and completed the operation.

When raising myself on my elbow I saw the head of a column of Federal troops about seventy-five yards toward our right front, advancing obliquely toward us. I was horrified, jumped up and exclaimed to Douthat: "What are you doing?" as he faced in their direction. He dropped his gun and answered: "It's time to get away from here," and I started on the run behind him, as we both rapidly retired from the advancing foes. We made good time getting away, and got some distance before they opened fire on us--perhaps 100 or 150 yards. We ran out of range, shot after shot falling around us, until we got over the Emmettsburg road toward our lines. After we had got over the fences along the road the fire didn't disturb us. No organized body of troops did I meet in going back. I wondered how few I saw in this retreat from the hill top. I reached ere long the tent of a friend, Captain Charles M. Blackford, judge advocate of our Second Corps, at Longstreet's headquarters, and this was the last of the battle of Gettysburg time. I didn't hear of Lieutenant-Colonel Otey being wounded until after the battle was over, though I have since understood it was shortly after the advance commenced. I, the Captain of Company G, was the only commissioned officer with the company that day. I may properly mention an incident or two.

WOUNDED.

Now the battery of the descending slope was advanced. Sergeant James R. Kent, of my company, suddenly plunged forward in a ditch, and I asked of him: "How are you hurt, Kent?" for I knew he was hit. He answered: "Shot through the leg." About the time we sent "Big Foot Walker" back for reinforcements, "Blackeyed Williams," as we called him, a private of my company, called to me: "Look here, Captain," at the same time pulling up his shirt at the back and showing a cut where a bullet had a full mark about its depth in the flesh. Quite a number of the men on the hill top had been struck one way or another, and there were many nursing and tying up their wounds. Kent's leg had been fractured--the small bone--and he was captured.

Before an advance I went several times to the crest where our artillery was planted, and could see the enemy in our front throwing up dirt on the line which we afterwards took. Just before the cannonade commenced Major James Downing rode along the line of guns in our immediate front, carrying a flag.

PERSONAL.

I came away from Longstreet's headquarters after spending the night (after the battle in Captain Blackford's tent) in a wagon with a long train of wagons that carried one to Williamsport, leaving about noon and traveling through the next night. Next morning we reached Williamsport. The town was attacked at several points, but not where I was.

Captain William Early--or Lieutenant Early, as he was then--I met at Williamsport as I got out of the wagons, and asked me to dinner. I told him I couldn't walk, for I was sore and stiff, and he went off to get me a horse. But he didn't return, and I did not see him again, for just then his guns opened and a lively skirmish ensued, but soon quieted down. After remaining a few hours on the north side of the river, a big ferry boat was brought up, and, having collected fifty or sixty of the

11th Virginia infantry who were wounded, I took charge of them and carried them on the boat across the river that evening. Then we marched next morning for Winchester, reaching there in two days. I did not see my regiment in the campaign after the fight. In a few months my leg healed and I rejoined my regiment at Hanover junction in the fall.

The above is correct.

Jno. Holmes Smith,

Late Captain Company G, Home Guards,

of Lynchburg, Va.

(Source: Southern Historical Society Papers, Vol. 32, pages 183-195)

From the Times-Dispatch, May 6, 1906.

PICKETT'S CHARGE AT GETTYSBURG.

Graphic Story Told by Late Colonel Joseph C. Mayo,

Third Virginia Regiment.

Why Don't They Support Us--Why the "Unknown

Private Beyond" Had to Be Killed That Day.

Richmond, Va., April 24, 1906.

Editor of The Times-Dispatch:

Sir,--I send you an account of Gettysburg by the late Col. Joseph Mayo, of the Third Virginia Infantry, Kemper's brigade. This gallant officer was a Virginia Military Institute man, and like every other field officer of Pickett's division, without a single exception, he was stricken in the dreadful assault. It has sometimes been said that all of Pickett's field officers were wounded except Major Joseph C. Cabell, of Danville. This is a mistake. He was also shot in the charge, though not severely.

It was stated that Col. Eppa Hunton, of the Eighth Virginia Infantry, Garnett's brigade, rode his hose through the action until both he and his horse were shot. Having his painful wound attended, he turned to ride forward again when his horse fell dead.

The account is a graphic one and bears the impress of truth.

Col. J.B. Batchelder, in his account of Gettysburg, states that Pickett's men chased the enemy beyond the point where Armistead fell.

Col. Mayo's account tells the story of a private who fell twenty paces beyond that point. Co. Mayo some years since passed over the river. His surviving comrades will read with interest the story of their deeds from his pen.

Very truly yours,

Jno. W. Daniel.

PICKETT'S CHARGE AT GETTYSBURG.

The order of march into the enemy's country was left in front; first Ewell's, then Hill's, and, lastly, Longstreet's corps, of which Armistead's, Garnett's and Kemper's brigades of Pickett's Division, brought up the rear. The other two brigades, those of Corse and Jenkins, were absent on detached service. We reached Chambersburg early on the evening of June 27th, and stayed there until hastily summoned to the scene of hostilities on the morning of the 2d of July, having been employed in the meantime, in tearing up the railroad track and demolishing the depot and other buildings. A forced march of twenty-five miles brought us, at about 3 o'clock in the afternoon, to the stone bridge on the Cashtown and Gettysburg Turnpike, within cannon shot of the battle-field. Here General Pickett sent Col. Walter Harrison, of his staff, to tell General Lee of our arrival and readiness for action.

THE POST OF HONOR, JULY 3rd.

The answer came to find a camp and await further orders. Before dawn the following morning, we moved to our place in the line, our march being carefully concealed from the enemy's view. Soon after we got into position, some two hundred yards in the rear of the batteries on Seminary Ridge, General Lee passed in front of us, coming from the right, and a little while afterwards every man in the ranks was made to know exactly what was the work which had been cut out for us. I remember perfectly well General Kemper's earnest injunction to me to be sure that the Third Virginia was told that the commanding general had assigned our division the post of honor that day. He was a Virginian; so were they. Then the arms were stacked and the men allowed to rest at will; but one thing was especially noticeable; from being unusually merry and hilarious they on a sudden had become as still and thoughtful as Quakers at a love feast. Walking up the line to where Colonel Patton was standing in front of the Seventh, I said to him, "This news has brought about an awful seriousness with our fellows, Taz." "Yes," he replied, "and well they may be serious if they really know what is in store for them. I have been up yonder where Dearing is, and looked across at the Yankees."

Then he told me a good joke he had on our dashing and debonair chief of artillery. He had ridden out on the skirmish line to get a closer observation of the enemy's position, when a courier galloped up with a message from General Lee. Naturally he supposed Mars Robert wished to ask him what he had seen of those people that was worth reporting; but he was woefully mistaken. This was all the General had to say: "Major Dearing, I do not approve of young officers needlessly exposing themselves; your place is with your batteries." While we were talking an order came to move up nearer the artillery. This was done, and the final preparations made for the advance. Here let me say that General Kemper's memory was at fault when he said in his letter to Judge David E. Johnston, dated February 4, 1886, that he and General Garnett were the only officers of Pickett's Division who went into that battle mounted. He himself gave Col. Lewis B. Williams, of the First, permission to keep his horse, as he was too unwell to walk, and after the General was shot down I saw two of his staff, Captain William O. Fry and Orderly Walker, still on horseback.

THE TEMPEST AT 1 O'CLOCK.

Meantime the blazing sun had reached and passed the meridian, and the long, painful interval of suspense is swallowed up in the excruciating reality. Where the Third and the greater part of the Seventh lay there was a depression in the ridge, exposing them to the full fury of the tempest of shot and shell which soon came raining down upon them. A faint conception of its indescribable horror may be gathered from a few incidents of which I retain to this day a shuddering recollection. At the sound of the signal guns I went to the centre of the regiment in front of the flag, and sat down upon a pile of blankets resembling a coil of rope; but the intolerable heat of the sun quickly drove me back to the shelter of the apple tree, under which men and officers of both regiments were crowded together thick as herring in a barrel, where I managed to squeeze in between Colonel Patton and Colonel Collcote.

PANDEMONIUM.

The first shot or two flew harmlessly over our heads; but soon they began to get the range, and then came--well, what General Gibbon, on the other side, called "pandemonium." First there was an explosion in the top of our friendly tree, sending a shower of limbs upon us. In a second there was another, followed by a piercing shriek, which caused Patton to spring up and run to see what was the matter. Two killed outright and three frightfully wounded, he said on his return. Immediately after a like cry came from another apple tree close by in the midst of the Third. Company F had suffered terribly; First Lieutenant A.P. Gomer, legs shattered below the knee; of the Arthur brothers, second and third lieutenants, one killed and the other badly hit; Orderly Sergeant Murray mortally wounded, and of the privates, one killed and three wounded. Then, for more than an hour it went on. Nearly every minute the cry of mortal agony was heard above the roar and rumble of the guns. In his modest book, "Four Years a Soldier," one who was left for dead under that apple tree describes it in these feeling words: "Turn you where you would, there was to be seen at almost every moment of time guns, swords, haversacks, human flesh and bones flying and dangling in the air or bouncing above the earth, which now trembled beneath us as shaken by an earthquake. Over us, in front of us, behind us, in our midst and through our ranks, poured solid shot and bursting shell dealing out death on every hand; yet the men stood bravely at their post in an open field with a blistering July sun beating upon their unprotected heads." Doubtless there would have been some consolation to know, as we afterwards learned, that our blue-coated friends over the way were in the same, if not a worse predicament. General Gibbon who with Hancock's Corps held the position we were about to storm says of the execution done by our batteries that it exceeded anything he had dreamed of in artillery warfare; and I believe it is now an admitted historical fact that from the time that the "nimble gunner with limestock the devilish cannon touched," that awful din at Gettysburg was the most fearful sound that ever pealed from the "red throat of roaring war." Colonel Patton called my attention to the gallant bearing of Major Dearing, as he galloped, flag in hand, from gun to gun of his battalion and suggested that it would be safer for us to close up on the artillery; but I told him he must not think of moving without orders and, besides, it was evident that the enemy's fire was rapidly abating, and that the storm would soon be over. The words were barely spoken before it came again; our turn now. I thought at first that it was my adjutant, John Stewart, as a handful of earth mixed with blood and brains struck my shoulder; but they were two poor fellows belonging to Company D (one of them, I remember, had a flaming red head), and another, as we believed, mortally hurt, Sergeant-Major Davy Johnston, of the Seventh, author of the book I have quoted. Strange to say, he was at the time lying between Colonel Patton, and myself.

"REMEMBER OLD VIRGINIA."

That was among the last shots fired, and as the terrific duel was drawing to a close, General Pickett came riding briskly down the rear of the line, calling to the men to get up and prepare to advance, and "Remember Old Virginia." Our dear old Third, it was a heart-rending sight which greeted me as I moved along your decimated ranks!--while quickly, and without a word of command, the men fell into their places; especially to see our color-bearer, Murden, as fine a type of true soldier-ship as ever stepped beneath the folds of the spotless stars and bars, now lying there stark and stiff, a hideous hole sheer through his stalwart body, and his right hand closed in a death grip around the staff of that beautiful new flag which to-day for the first and last time had braved the battle and the breeze. The devoted little column moved to the assault, with Garnett, and Kemper in front, and Armistead behind in close supporting distance. Soon after clearing our batteries it was found necessary to change direction to the left. While conducting the movement, which was made in perfect order under a galling flank fire from the Round Top, General Pickett, for the second time, cautioned me to be sure and keep the proper interval with General Garnett; Armistead was expected to catch up and extend the line to the left. Then we swept onward again, straight for the Golgotha of Seminary Ridge, half a mile distant, across the open plain. As we neared the Emmettsburg road, along which, behind piles of rails, the enemy's strong line of skirmishers was posted, General Kemper called to me to give attention to matters on the left, while he went to see what troops those were coming up behind us. Glancing after him, I caught a glimpse of a small body of men, compact and solid as a wedge, moving swiftly to the left oblique, as if aiming to uncover Garnett's Brigade. They were Armistead's people, and as Kemper cantered down their front on his mettlesome sorrel they greeted him with a rousing cheer, which I know made his gallant heart leap for joy. At the same moment I saw a disorderly crowd of men breaking for the rear, and Pickett, with Stuart Symington, Ned Baird, and others, vainly trying to stop the rout. And now the guns of Cushing and Abbott double-stocked by General Gibbon's express order, reinforced the terrific fire of the infantry behind the stone fence, literally riddling the orchard on the left of the now famous Cordori house, through which my regiment and some of the others passed.

"DON'T CROWD, BOYS"--"PRETTY HOT"--"PERFECTLY RIDICULOUS"

While clearing this obstruction, and as we were getting into shape again, several things were impressed on my memory. First, the amusement it seemed to afford Orderly Waddy Forward, who might, if he pleased, have stayed behind with the horses, to see me duck my head as a ball whizzed in an ace of my nose; next, to see Captain Lewis, of Company C, looking as lazy and lackadaisical, and, if possible, more tired and bored than usual, carrying his sword point foremost over his shoulder, and addressing his company in that invariable plaintive tone, half command, half entreaty, "Don't crowd, boys; don't crowd." "Pretty hot, Captain," I said in passing. "It's redicklous, Colonel; perfectly redicklous"-- which, in his vocabulary, meant as bad as bad could be; then Captain Tom Hodges directed my attention to a splendid looking Federal officer, magnificently mounted, straining his horse at full speed along the crest of a hill a hundred yards in our front, and both of us calling to the skirmishers, "Don't shoot him! don't shoot him!" and, lastly, the impetuous Kemper, as rising in his stirrups and pointing to the left with his sword, he shouted, "There are the guns, boys, go for them." It was an injudicious order; but they obeyed with a will, and mingled with Garnett's people pushed rapidly up the heights.

Within a few steps of the stone fence, while in the act of shaking hands with General Garnett and congratulating him on being able to be with his men (he had been seriously ill a few days before), I heard some one calling me, and turning my head, saw that it was Captain Fry. He was mounted, and blood streaming from his horse's neck. Colonel Terry had sent him to stop the rush to left. The enemy in force (Stannard's Vermonters) had penetrated to our rear. He told me that Kemper had been struck down, it was feared mortally. With the help of Colonel Carrington, of the Eighteenth, and Major Bentley, of the Twenty-fourth, I hastily gathered a small band together and faced them to meet the new danger. After that everything was a wild kaleidoscopic whirl. A man near me seemed to be keeping a tally of the dead for my especial benefit. First it was Patton, then Collcote, then Phillips, and I know not how many more. Colonel Williams was knocked out of the saddle by a ball in the shoulder near the brick-house, and in falling was killed by his sword. His little bay mare kept on with the men in the charge. I can see her now as she came limping and sadly crippled down the hill. I saw her again at Williamsport in care of his faithful man Harry, who asked me what I thought old master would say when she was all belonging to Mars Lewis he had to take home. Seeing the men as they fired, throw down their guns and pick up others from the ground, I followed suit, shooting into a flock of blue coats that were pouring down from the right, I noticed how close their flags were together. Probably they were the same people whom Hood and McLaws had handled so roughly the day before. "Used up," as General Meade said of them. Suddenly there was a hissing sound, like the hooded cobra's whisper of death, a deafening explosion, a sharp pang of pain somewhere, a momentary blank, and when I got on my feet again there were splinters of bone and lumps of flesh sticking to my clothes. Then I remembered seeing lank Tell Taliaferro, adjutant of the Twenty-fourth, jumping like a kangaroo and rubbing his crazy bone and blessing the Yankees in a way that did credit to old Jube Early's one-time law partner, and handsome Ocey White, the boy lieutenant of Company A, taking off his hat to show me where a ball had raised a whelk on his scalp and carried away one of his pretty flaxen curls, and lastly, "Old Buck" Terry, with a peculiarly sad smile on his face, standing with poor George and Val Harris and others, between the colors of the Eleventh and Twenty-fourth, near where now is the pretty monument of colonel Ward, of Massachusetts. I could not hear what he said, but he was pointing rearwards with his sword, and I knew what that meant.

As I gave one hurried glance over the field we had traversed, the thought in my mind was repeated at my side, "Oh! Colonel, why don't they support us?" It was Walker, General Kemper's orderly, unhorsed, but still unscathed and undaunted, awkward, ungainly, hard-featured, good-natured, simple-minded, stout-hearted Walker, one of the Eleventh boys, I believe; only a private doing his duty with might and main and recking no more of glory than the ox that has won the prize at a cattle show. At the storming of the Redan when Wyndham's forlorn hope tumbled into the ditch and couldn't get out, owing to the scarcity of ladders, and the few they had were too short, the men huddled together dazed and bewildered, and were mowed down like dumb beasts by the Muscovite rifles, because there were no officers left to lead them. There was a notable exception, an Irishman, scrambling up the scrap, he shouted, "Come up, boys, follow the captain." The captain fell, but Pat went on to immortality. It was not so that day at Gettysburg.

UNKNOWN PRIVATE WHO FELL BEYOND.

Twenty paces beyond the spot which is marked to tell where stout old Armistead fell, the foremost hero of them all, a humble private, without a name, bit the dust. The man in blue who told the story had a seam in his cheek. "I tried to save him, but he would not give up, so I had to kill him to save my own life." "What orders do you leave us, my lord, if you are killed?" asked Hill of Wellington when the pounding was hardest on the famous plateau at Waterloo. "Do as I am doing," he replied, and turning to the men, he said, "Boys, you can't think of giving way. Remember old England." And well it was for old England that behind the Iron Duke was a wall of iron men. Calling to the group around me to spread themselves, I led the way back to the woods in rear of our guns on Seminary Ridge. Realizing painfully our own sad plight, we were, of course, anxiously concerned for the rest of our people. But soon Mars Robert came along, followed by his faithful aides, the two Charleses --Venable and Marshall. How ineffably grand he appeared--a very anointed king of command, posing for the chisel of a Phidias, and looking on him we knew that the army was safe.

So ended our part in the day's bloody work.

[From the Richmond, Va., Times-Dispatch, February 7,1904.]

PICKETT'S CHARGE.

The Story of It as Told by a Member of His Staff

CAPTAIN ROBERT A. BRIGHT.

Statements to Where the General Was During the Charge.--Why the Attack Failed.

The following statement of what I saw and heard on the third day at Gettysburg was in the main written about thirty years ago, and was rewritten for publication in 1903, but the issue of it was prevented until now by an attack of gout, from which I suffered. I earnestly wish that it had come out before the death of my corps commander, the brave General Longstreet.

Early in the morning Pickett's Virginians, forty-seven hundred muskets, with officers added, five thousand strong, moved from the camping ground of the second day, two miles in rear, to the battlefield, and took position behind the hill from which we charged later in the day. Then came the order from headquarters: "Colonel E. P. Alexander will command the entire artillery in action to-day, and Brigadier-General Pendleton will have charge of the reserve artillery ammunition of the army." Later, General Pickett was informed from General Longstreet's headquarters that Colonel Alexander would give the order when the charge should begin. Several hours later the batteries on both sides opened. Had this occurred at night, it would have delighted the eye more than any fire works ever seen.

ENGLISH GORDON.

Shortly before the artillery duel commenced, I returned from looking over the ground in our front, and found General Pickett talking to a strange officer, to whom he introduced me saying: "This is Colonel Gordon, once opposed to me in the San Juan affair, but now on our side."

In explanation of this I will state here that the San Juan affair occurred on the Pacific coast when General Pickett was captain in the United States army, and when he held the island against three English ships of war and 1,000 English regulars, he having one company of United States infantry and part of another company. General Winfield Scott was sent out by this government to settle the trouble.

After the introduction, Colonel Gordon, who was an Englishman, continued speaking to General Pickett, and said:

"Pickett, my men are not going up to-day."

The General said--

"But, Gordon, they must go up; you must make them go up."

Colonel Gordon answered:

"You know, Pickett, I will go as far with you as any other man, if only for old acquaintance sake, but my men have until lately been down at the seashore, only under the fire of heavy guns from ships, but for the last day or two they have lost heavily under infantry fire and are very sore, and they will not go up to-day."

This officer was on foot, there was no horse in sight, and he must have come from Pettigrew's Brigade on our left, only some 200 yards distant.

I have written and asked about the command to which this officer belonged, but have met with no success.

Three times General Pickett sent to Colonel Alexander, asking: "Is it time to charge?" The last messenger brought back this answer: "Tell General Pickett I think we have silenced eight of the enemy's guns, and now is the thee to charge." (Some Federal officers after the war informed me that they had only run these guns back to cool.)

MOUNTED OFFICERS.

General Pickett ordered his staff-officers, four in number (Major Charles Pickett, Captain Baird, Captain Symington and myself), to Generals Armistead, Garnett and Kemper, and to Dearing's Artillery Battalion, which earlier in the day had been ordered to follow up the charge and keep its caissons full. Orders to the other staff officers I did not hear. But I was sent to General Kemper with this order:

"You and your staff and field officers to go in dismounted; dress on Garnett and take the red barn for your objective point."

During the charge I found Kemper and Garnett apparently drifting too much to the left, and I believe it was because the red barn was too much to Kemper's left. General Pickett would have altered the direction, but our left being exposed by the retreat of Pettigrew's command, our men and 10,000 more were needed to the left.

When I reached General Kemper, he stood up, removing a handkerchief from under his hat, with which he had covered his face to keep the gravel knocked up by the fierce artillery fire from his eyes. As I gave the order, Robert McCandlish Jones, a friend and schoolmate of mine, called out: "Bob, turn us loose and we will take them." Then Colonel Lewis Williams, of the 1st Virginia Regiment, came to me and said: "Captain Bright, I wish to ride my mare up," and I answered: "Colonel Williams, you cannot do it. Have you not just heard me give the order to your general to go up on foot ?" and he said: "But you will let me ride; I am sick to-day, and besides that, remember Williamsburg." Now Williamsburg was my home and I remembered that Colonel Williams had been shot through the shoulder in that battle and left at Mrs. Judge Tucker's house on the courthouse green. This I had heard, for I missed that fight, so I answered: "Mount your mare and I will make an excuse for you." General Garnett had been injured by a kick while passing through the wagon train at night, had been allowed to ride; Colonel Hunton of the same brigade also rode, being unable to walk. He fell on one side of the red barn and General Kemper on the other side.

So there were eight mounted officers, counting General Pickett and staff, mounted in the charge.

Colonel Williams fell earlier in the fight. His mare went up rideless almost to the stone wall and was caught when walking back by Captain William C. Marshall, of Dearing's Battalion. His own horse, Lee, having been killed, he rode Colonel Williams' mare away after the fight. When I returned to General Pickett from giving the order to General Kemper, Symington, Baird and Charles Pickett were with the General, they having less distance to carry their orders than I, as Kemper was on our right, and Armistead not in first line, but in echelon.

WHERE PICKETT WAS.

The command had moved about fifty yards in the charge. General Pickett and staff were about twenty yards in rear of the column.

When we had gone about four hundred yards the General said: "Captain, you have lost your spurs to-day, instead of gaining them." Riding on the right side, I looked at once at my left boot, and saw that the shank of my spur had been mashed around and the rowel was looking towards the front, the work of a piece of shell, I suppose, but that was the first I knew of it. Then I remembered the Irishman's remark, that one spur was enough, because if one side of your horse went, the other would be sure to go.

When we had charged about 750 yards, having about 500 more to get over before reaching the stone wall, Pettigrew's Brigade broke all to pieces and left the field in great disorder. At this time we were mostly under a fierce artillery fire; the heaviest musketry fire came farther on.

General Pettigrew was in command that day of a division and his brigade was led by Colonel Marshall, who was knocked from his horse by a piece of shell as his men broke, but he had himself lifted on his horse, and when his men refused to follow him up, he asked that his horse be turned to the front. Then he rode up until. he was killed. If all the men on Pickett's left had gone on like Marshall, history would have been written another way. General Pickett sent Captain Symington and Captain Baird to rally these men.

They did all that brave officers could do, but could not stop the stampede.

LONGSTREET AND FREEMANTLE.

General Pickett directed me to ride to General Longstreet and say that the position against which he had been sent would be taken, but he could not hold it unless reiforcements be sent to him. As I rode back to General Longstreet I passed small parties of Pettigrew's command going to the rear; presently I came to quite a large squad, and, very foolishly, for I was burning precious time, I halted them, and asked if they would not go up and help those gallant men now charging behind us. Then I added, "What are you running for?" and one of them, looking up at me with much surprise depicted on his face, said. "Why, good gracious, Captain, ain't you running yourself?" Up to the present time I`have not answered that question, but will now say, appearances were against me.

I found General Longstreet sitting on a fence alone; the fence ran in the direction we were charging. Pickett's column had passed over the hill on our side of the Emmettsburg road, and could not then be seen. I delivered the message as sent by General Pickett. General Longstreet said: "Where are the troops that were placed on your flank ?" and I answered: "Look over your shoulder and you will see them." He looked and saw the broken fragments. Just then an officer rode at half-speed, drawing up his horse in front of the General, and saying: "General Longstreet, General Lee sent me here, and said you would place me in a position to see this magnificent charge. I would not have missed it for the world." General Longstreet answered: "I would, Colonel Freemantle, the charge is over. Captain Bright, ride to General Pickett, and tell hin what you have heard me say to Colonel Freemantle." At this moment our men were near to but had not crossed the Emmettsburg road. I started and when my horse had made two leaps, General Longstreet called: "Captain Bright!" I checked my horse, and turned half around in my saddle to hear, and this was what he said: "Tell General Pickett that Wilcox's Brigade is in that peach orchard (pointing), and he can order him to his assistance."

WILCOX AND PICKETT.

Some have claimed that Wilcox was put in the charge at its commencement--General Gordon says this; but this is a mistake. When I reached General Pickett he was at least one hundred yards behind the division, having been detained in a position from which he could watch and care for his left flank. He at once sent Captain Baird to General Wilcox with the order for him to come in; then he sent Captain Symington with the same order, in a very few moments, and last he said: "Captain Bright, you go,' and I was about the same distance behind Symington that he was behind Baird. The fire was so dreadful at this time that I believe that General Pickett thought not more than one out of the three sent would reach General Wilcox.

When I rode up to Wilcox he was standing with both hands raised waving and saying to me, "I know, I know." I said, "But, General, I must deliver my message." After doing this I rode out of the peach orchard, going forward where General Pickett was watching his left. Looking that way myself, I saw moving out of the enemy's line of battle, in head of column, a large force; having nothing in their front, they came around our flank as described above. Had our left not deserted us these men would have hesitated to move in head of column, confronted by a line of battle. When I reached General Pickett I found him too far down towards the Ennmettshurg road to see these flanking troops, and he asked of me the number. I remember answering 7,000, but this proved an over estimate. Some of our men had been faced to meet this new danger, and so doing somewhat broke the force of our charge on the left. Probably men of the 1st Virginia will remember this.

ARTILLERY AMMUNITION OUT.

I advised the General to withdraw his command before these troops got down far enough to left face, come into line of battle, sweep around our flank and shut us up. He said, "I have been watching my left all the time, expecting this, but it is provided for. Ride to Dearing's Battalion; they have orders to follow up the charge and keep their caissons filled; order them to open with every gun and break that column and keep it broken." The first officer I saw on reaching the battalion was Captain William C. Marshall (Postoffice, Morgantown, West Virginia). I gave him the order with direction to pass it down at once to the other three batteries. Marshall said: "The battalion has no ammunition. I have only three solid shot." I then asked why orders to keep caissons filled had not been obeyed, and he answered, "The caissons had been away nearly three-quarters of an hour, and there was a rumor that General Pendleton had sent the reserve artillery ammunition more than a mile in rear of the field." I directed him to open with his solid shot, but I knew all hope of halting the column was over, because solid shot do not halt columns. The second shot struck the head of column, the other two missed, and the guns were silent.

I found General Pickett in front about 300 yards ahead of the artillery position, and to the left of it, and some 200 yards behind the command which was then at the stone wall over which some of our men were going, that is, the 53rd Regiment, part of Armistead's Brigade, led by Colonel Rawley Martin, who fell next to the gallant General Armistead, had reached the enemy's guns and captured them. All along the stone wall, as far as they extended, Kemper and Garnett's men were fighting with but few officers left.

THE RETREAT--LEE'S REMARK.

I informed the General that no help was to be expected from the artillery, but the enemy were closing around us, and nothing could now save his command. He had remained behind to watch and protect that left, to put in first help expected from infantry supports, then to break the troops which came around his flank with the artillery; all had failed. At this moment our left (Pickett's Division) began to crumble and soon all that was left came slowly back, 5,000 in the morning, 1,600 were put in camp that night, 3,400 killed, wounded and missing.

We moved back, and when General Pickett and I were about 300 yards from the position from which the charge had started, General Robert E. Lee, the Peerless, alone, on Traveler, rode up and said: "General Pickett, place your division in rear of this hill, and be ready to repel the advance of the enemy should they follow up their advantage." (I never heard General Lee call them the enemy before; it was always those or these people). General Pickett, with his head on his breast, said: "General Lee, I have no division now, Armistead is down, Garnett is down, and Kemper is mortally wounded."

Then General Lee said: "Come, General Pickett, this has been my fight and upon my shoulders rests the blame. The men and officers of your command have written the name of Virginia as high to-day as it has ever been written before." (Now talk about "Glory enough for one day," why this was glory enough for one hundred years.)

LEE AND KEMPER.

Then turning to me, General Lee said: Captain, what officer is that they are bearing off?" I answered, "General Kemper," and General Lee said: "I must speak to him," and moved Traveler towards the litter. I moved my horse along with his, but General Pickett did not go with us. The four bearers, seeing it was General Lee, halted, and General Kemper, feeling the halt, opened his eyes. General Lee said: "General Kemper, I hope you are not very seriously wounded."

General Kemper answered: "I am struck in the groin, and the ball has ranged upwards; they tell me it is mortal;" and General Lee said: "I hope it will not prove so bad as that; is there anything I can do for you, General Kemper?" The answer came, after General Kemper had, seemingly with much pain, raised himself on one elbow:

"Yes, General Lee, do full justice to this division for its work to-day."

General Lee bowed his head, and said: "I will."

I wish to mention here that Captain William I. Clopton, now judge of Manchester, told me after the war that while General Pickett was trying to guard his left, he saw twenty-seven battleflags, each with the usual complement of men, move out on our right flank, but we did not see this, as all our thoughts were fixed on our left flank.

Captain Symington and Captain Baird could each give many interesting incidents if they could be induced to write for publication. My article of the 10th of December, 1903, in The Times-Dispatch, should be read before this account, to show how and when General Pickett's command reached Gettysburg.

PERSONAL

Should I write again, it will be about the 4,000 prisoners we guarded back to Virginia, Kemper's supposed death bed, and General Lee's note to Pickett a few days after Gettysburg. To those seeking the truth about this great battle, I will say, the very great losses in other commands occurred on the first and second days. The third day, at this exhibition, was most decidedly Virginia day, and a future Virginia Governor, Kemper by name, was present. I wish here to state that some of the men of Garnett's Brigade told me they saw up at the stone wall, fighting with them, some men and officers, mostly the latter, of two other States, and in answer to my questions as to numbers and organization, answered, numbering in all, less than sixty, and without formation of any military kind, Alabamians and North Carolinians.

Now, as to the position of Armistead's Brigade in the charge. He was ordered to go in on the left of Garnett, but Captain Winfree, a most gallant officer of the 14th Virginia, now living in this city, agrees with my memory, that Armistead's brigade went in between Garnett and Kemper. I also wish to give such information as I can to Senator Daniel, who asked for it in the Confederate column of Sunday's Times-Dispatch, 24th of January, about the losses of Pickett's three brigades on the third day. No official returns came to us until long after the battle, because no one was left to make the report, and hardly any one was left to receive such report. General Pickett's staff officers who encamped the command on the night of the third day counted sixteen hundred. I find Senator Daniel since the war always turning from Washington to Virginia, like the needle to the pole, but, strange to say, during the war I found him always turning from Virginia to Washington as though he wanted that city.

Very respectfully, Ro. A. BRIGHT,

Formerly on the staff of Major-General George E. Pickett.

(Source: Southern Historical Society Papers, Vol. 31, p.228-236)

GENERAL ARMISTEAD'S PORTRAIT PRESENTED.

An Address Delivered Before R. E. Lee Camp No. 1,

C.V., Richmond, Va., January 29, 1909.

By Rev. JAMES E. POINDEXTER, Late Captain in 38th Virginia

Regiment, Armistead's Brigade, Pickett's Division.

Mr. Commander and Comrades:

It was my wish that this address should be made by Col. Rawley W. Martin, of Lynchburg, who led the Fifty-third Virginia in Pickett's charge, and fell by the side of Armistead on Cemetery Ridge. But this could not be, and so I come to take his place. For the task assigned me I feel myself but poorly equipped. Unlike Col. Martin, I followed our old Commander, as St. Peter followed the Master, "afar off." It is, I may say, with unfeigned diffidence that I venture to speak of war to the veteran soldiers who are here to-night.

On me, however, through your kindness, is this honor conferred, that I should present to the Camp the portrait of Lewis A. Armistead. I thank you for it with all my heart.

The Armistead family, coming direct from England, settled in Virginia in 1636, and became ere long a family of soldiers. Five brothers, three of them in the regular army, took part in the war of 1812. Col. George Armistead, the oldest of the five, defended Fort McHenry. The flag which waved over it during the bombardment, which Key immortalized as the "Star Spangled Banner," was long guarded as a sacred heir-loom by his descendants. It is now laid up in the National Museum. A second brother, Lewis Gustavus Adolphus, named for the Swedish hero, "The Lion of the North," fell at Fort Erie. Walker Keith Armistead, the father of our old chief, graduated at West Point in 1803, fought in Canada, closed the Seminole war, and was, when he died in 1845, second in command in the regular army. Miss Stanley, who became his wife, was a native of the old North State, and so it happened that Lewis A. Armistead was born at Newbern, N. C., in 1817.

As a matter of course, the young Lewis entered West Point in 1836. Here, however, his career was cut short. He became involved in a personal conflict with Jubal A. Early, who had insulted him on the parade ground, and cracking the worthy's head with a mess-hall plate, as the story runs, was retired from West Point; but in 1839 entered the regular army as lieutenant in the Sixth Regiment of Infantry, and fought against the Seminoles under Zachary Taylor and under his own father. During the war with Mexico he did splendid service. He led the storming party at Chapultepec, and was brevetted Captain and then Major for gallantry displayed at Contreras, and Cherubusco, and Molino Del Ray. That war being ended, he served for fourteen years on the frontier, and in 1859 marched against the hostile Indians and defeated them.

On the secession of Virginia he promptly resigned his command in the old army, tramped on foot across the plains to Austin, Texas, came straight to Richmond, and in April, 1861, was made Colonel of the Fifty-seventh Virginia, and twelve months afterwards, in April, 1862, was commissioned Brigadier-General. In that capacity he fought at Seven Pines, at Malvern Hill, at Second Manassas, at Sharpsburg, displaying everywhere conspicuous gallantry, and winning by his coolness under fire, by his stern perseverance and his indomitable pluck, the applause of his superiors and the entire confidence of his men.

During the first Maryland campaign he was made Provost Marshal of the army, and received the personal thanks of General Lee for the ability with which he discharged the duties of that office.

In September, 1862, his brigade, which comprised the Fifty-seventh, Fifty-third, the Fourteenth, the Ninth and the Thirty-eighth Virginia, was incorporated with Pickett's Division.

General Armistead was no "holiday soldier," no "carpet-knight." "He was," says Col. Martin, "a strict disciplinarian, but never a martinet. Obedience to duty he regarded as the first qualification of a soldier. For straggling on the march on neglect of duty on the part of his men, he held the officer in immediate command strictly responsible. The private must answer to the officer, but the officer to him."

Thus far we have followed his career. Born of noble stock, a Virginian to his heart's core, linked by ties of blood with many of our best, the son of a soldier, familiar from childhood with tales of war, trained at West Point, tested by years of service in Florida, in Texas, in Mexico, in Virginia, obedient to duty, demanding in turn obedience from others, resolute, unyielding, with courage tempered in the flame of battle, he waited for a fit opportunity to prove himself the hero he was, to write his name high on the roll of fame and win the plaudits of the world.

That opportunity came at Gettysburg. Of the charge made by Pettigrew and Pickett on Cemetery Ridge, I do not propose to speak at length. On the controversies which have raged around it, I shall not touch. But in order to appreciate the heroism of Armistead we must picture in few words the part played by Pickett's Division.

During the artillery duel which preceded the charge we lay quiet and (some of us) hugged the ground. When the cannonade subsided we fell in at the word of command and moved in line of battle over the wooded ridge in front, past our artillery, and down the slope to the edge of the woods. Here, for the first time, we caught sight of the field of battle. A thousand yards away lay Cemetery Ridge, curving around to the left to Culp's Hill, and off to our right stood Round-Top and little Round-Top, crowned with artillery. Beyond that ridge and on its crest lay eighty thousand men, every breastwork finished, every reserve posted, every gun in position, awaiting our assault. Between us and Cemetery Ridge was a field as open as this floor, not a treee, not a stone to shelter one man from the storm of battle. The scene which met the eyes of Armistead's men as we descended the slope was splendid. Before us, one hundred and fifty yards away, moving on like waves of the sea, marched Garnett and Kemper, their battle-flags flashing in the sunlight. The regiments of Armistead, marching in perfect order, with disciplined tread, followed where they led.

Soon the heavy guns on Round-Top were trained upon us, and howling shells burst around us or crashed through our ranks. The further we advanced the more tremendous was the cannonade. Our own artillery on the heights behind thundered over our heads at the enemy's guns on Cemetery Ridge. And so we marched "vaulted with fire."

As we crossed the plain beyond the Cordori house, we halted at the word of command, moved by the left flank, till opposite the point we aimed to strike, then in line of battle, the guns on Cemetery Ridge blazing in our faces, and every regiment of Armistead's brigade dressed on its colors as straight as the line of yonder door.

The gallant men who met our onset thrilled with emotions of fear and admiration--they tell it themselves--at the "grandeur" of the scene, at the "magnificence" of our advance. To the Count de Paris, as he watched the Confederate column bearing down all opposition, buffeting with unshaken courage the fierce volleys that met it, "it seemed," he says, "to be driven by an irresistible force."

Meanwhile the fire of the enemy grew every more violent, ever more destructive. The cannon on Round-Top "volleyed and thundered." From Cemetery Ridge grapeshot and canister tore through our ranks. We marched, says Longstreet, "through a fearful fire from the batteries in front and from Round-Top." "The slaughter," he says, "was terrible, the enfilade fire from batteries on Round-Top very destructive." But worse remained behind. From the stone wall which sheltered their ranks the hostile infantry "poured down," as Longstreet says, "a terrific fire." The hiss of bullets was incessant. Men fell at every step; they fell, I thought, like grass before the scythe.

Such were the scenes which some of us witnessed that day. The severity of our loss attests how deadly were the perils through which we passed. Of three Brigadiers, two were buried on the field, and one left weltering in his blood. Of the fifteen men who led the regiments of Pickett not one escaped. Seven were disabled, some with ghastly wounds, and eight of them were slain outright. Of all the field officers in the whole division only two remained unhurt. "It was a miracle," says the Count de Paris, "to see them safe and sound."

And now, bearing these things firmly in mind, let us follow Armistead. "A short time," says Col. Martin, "before the advance was ordered, the General, as his custom was, marched up and down in front of his troops, encouraging them in every way," for the shock of arms so soon to follow. "Remember, men, what you are fighting for. Remember your homes and your firesides, your mothers and wives and sisters and your sweethearts."

When the signal guns fired, he promptly called "attention," and instantly every man was on his feet. Coming then right to the front of the Fifty-third Virginia, which was that day the battalion of direction, he said to Color-Sergeant Blackburn; "Sergeant, are you going to plant those colors on the enemy's works over yonder?" "Yes, General," was the firm reply, "if mortal man can do it, I will." Then the chief exhorted his men to follow their colors and to remember the brave words of Sergeant Blackburn, and giving the command, "Battalion, forward; guide-centre, march," he placed himself in front of the Fifty-third Virginia, and, marching on foot, twenty yards ahead of his brigade, watched and directed our advance. It was not long before the battle was raging in all its fury.

The brigades of Garnett and Kemper were in our front, and as we drew near the advance lines Kemper rode back to Armistead, who marched on foot, and said: "Armistead, hurry up; I am going to charge those heights and carry them, and I want you to support me." "I'll do it," he replied. Then, glorying in the conduct of his men, he said to Kemper: "Look at my line; it never looked better on dress parade."

And now came the supreme test. He quietly gave the order, "Colonel, double-quick." And putting his black felt hat on the point of his sword, he led the advance, all the time in front of his line of battle, marching straight ahead through a hail of bullets, "the very embodiment of a heroic commander." The sword pierced through the hat, and more than once it slipped down to the hilt, and we saw above it the naked steel. As often as the hat slipped down the old hero would hoist it again to the sword's point. And so, born aloft with matchless courage, it caught the eye, it nerved the hearts of his devoted men, a standard as glorious, as worthy to be sung, as the plume that floated at Ivry above the helmet of Navarre.

And now the battle raged with redoubled fury. "As we got within forty yards of the stone wall," says Lieutenant Whitehead, "came all along the line the order of charge, and charge we did.

From behind the fence the Yankee infantry rose and poured into our ranks a murderous fire. Garnett's brigade and Kemper's had almost entirely disappeared; their brave commanders, their gallant officers, with hundred of the rank and file, were stretched on the field, and it remained for Armistead's men to finish the work. After a desperate fight the Yankees began to give way; and as they fell back our men rushed forward to the stone wall with unfaltering steps, Armistead still leading the charge."

The advance line halted here, but only for an instant. The veteran Armistead took in with the eye of a trained soldier the whole situation, and saw in a flash that to halt there meant ruin and defeat. Just ahead, bristling with cannon, was Cemetery Ridge. Just beyond it Hancock, "a foeman worthy of his steel," was hurrying up his heavy reserves. On the right and on the left the enemy's lines were still intact. On both flanks fierce assaults would soon be made on Pickett's men. "Colonel," said Armistead to the commanding officer of the Fifty-third, "we cannot stay here."

A word to Martin was enough. "Forward with the colors," he cried, and over the wall they went, Armistead and Martin; and with them went a gallant band resolved that day to conquer or die. The flag of the Fifty-third regiment, borne by Lieutenant Carter, flashed like a meteor in the van. The indomitable Armistead, his hat on the point of his sword, towered before them like a pillar of fire. "Follow me, boys; give them the cold steel." A hundred and fifty undaunted men followed their chief.

They left behind them the stone wall. They passed the earth works. They seized the cannon that, double shotted at ten yards distance, had torn our ranks with cannister. Victory seemed within their grasp. But alas! the support they looked for never came. In the nick of time Hancock's reserves were hurried to the front. They came on, he says, "four lines deep," and firing at close range, poured into the little band that followed Armistead a destructive volley. In that "hell of fire," as Bilharz says, "nothing could live." The intrepid Martin fell maimed for life. Forty-two of his brave Virginians lay dead around him. And there, in the Bloody Angle, our heroic chief, grasping a captured cannon to turn it on the foe, fell amongst his devoted men, pierced with mortal wounds, and sealing with his heart's blood the high-water mark of the Confederate cause.

As they bore him to the rear they met the gallant Hancock hurrying to the front.* [*A different account of this is given in Junkin's "Life of Hancock," page 117. I followed Colonel Martin.] Each recognized the other. They had been comrades in the old army. And learning who he was, Hancock dismounted, and grasping Armistead's hand, told him with a soldier's sympathy, how sorry he was to see him wounded, and promised to send mementoes and messages to his loved ones in Virginia, and tried to cheer him with the hope that his wounds would not be mortal, as our hero said. But Armistead was right. He knew that death was near at hand.

Carried from the field a prisoner, he lingered through the 4th of July and died on the 5th, "leaving," says Martin, "an example of patriotic ardor, of heroism and devotion to duty which ought to be handed down through the ages."

When his kinsmen heard of his glorious death they came and took his body, took all that was mortal of him, down to Baltimore, and with reverent hands laid him to rest amongst his own people, in the church-yard of old St. Paul's, the hero of Gettysburg besides the hero of Fort McHenry. A granite obelisk marks the spot where he fell on Cemetery Ridge. The sword which dropped from his dying grasp you may see it now in the Confederate Museum.

Such, comrades, was the soldier whose portrait we unveil tonight. As I stand before you my thoughts leap back over the forty-five years that lie between, back to the day when I saw him leading his brigade through the storm of shot and shell on the field of Gettysburg.

"None died on that field with greater glory than he, though many died, and there was much glory." Yes, comrades, we know how many died whose names we hold in deathless honor-- Edmonds and Owens, and Patton, and Williams, and Allen, and Stewart, and Hodges, and Magruder, and the knightly Garnett.

The heart of Virginia was wrung with anguish. Her stately head was bowed in grief. The flower of her chivalry fell in that fatal charge. But none fell so lamented as Armistead, none crowned the glory like his. Many others had done valiantly, but he surpassed them all. He did a deed that was matchless, unique, without a parallel on that field, when, leading his men with unflinching courage through the storm of fire, he pierced the enemy's line and fell there in the Bloody Angle. Not Wolfe at Quebec, not Ney at Waterloo, every exhibited a greater example of heroism and devotion than that displayed by our lamented chief.

The fame of his heroic deeds has spread through all the world. In every history they stand recorded. A generous foe unites with us to honor his memory. The stolid Longstreet kindles with enthusiasm to tell how "the noble Armistead fell on Cemetery Ridge by the wheels of the enemy's cannon."

And so, comrades, we present you now the portrait of a soldier, "without fear and withour reproach," of one who, tried with fiery trials, was always equal to the test; who, true as steel to his convictions, upheld on every field the honor of Virginia, and added yet another leaf to the chaplet of glory which shall forever encircle her queenly head. He comes to take his place in this "Hall of Fame" with the heroes of our heroic age, who leaped to arms forty-eight years ago, at the call of Virginia, and followed even unto death that starry cross which was to them the very symbol of duty and of self-sacrifice.

He comes to take his rightful place with Ashby and Pelham and Jackson, with Stuart and Pegram and A. P. Hill. They welcome him, this noble band, they hail him as a kindred spirit, as a comrade true. Our peerless Lee, we may well believe, looks with approval on this scene.

Long may that portrait hang upon these walls. May it show to all the word what men they were who followed once the banner of Lee. And if ever again the youth of Virginia are called to contend on the field of battle for her honor and her rights, may one glance at that noble face nerve their hearts with unflinching determination to do or die in her defence.

Hail then, unconquered chief, "Dead" once, like Latour d'Auvergne, "on the field of honor." We welcome thee to thy predestined place, "numbered now among the immortals."

(Source: Southern Historical Society Papers, Vol. 37, pp.144-151)

Bibliography

Boritt, Gabor S. (ed.). *Why the Confederacy Lost*. New York: Oxford University Press, 1992.

Catton, Bruce. *Grant Takes Command*. New York: Little, Brown and Company, 1968.

Collins, Donald E. *War Crime or Justice? General George Pickett and the Mass Execution of Deserters in Civil War Kinston, North Carolina*. Accessed via: http://homepages.rootsweb.ancestry.com/~ncuv/kinston1.htm 10.01.2012.

Doubleday, Abner. *Chancellorsville and Gettysburg*. New York: Da Capo Press, 1994.

Eicher, John H., and David J. Eicher. *Civil War High Commands*. Stanford, CA: Stanford University Press, 2001.

Find-a-Grave website, George Edward Pickett Grave: http://www.findagrave.com/cgi-bin/fg.cgi?GRid=812&page=gr accessed 09.29.2012.

Gaffney, P. and D. Gaffney. *The Civil War: Exploring History One Week at a Time*. New York: Hyperion, 2011.

Gardner, *The Memoirs of Brigadier General William Passmore Carlin, U. S. A.* Nebraska: University of Nebraska Press (1999).

Gordon, Lesley J. "The Seeds of Disaster: The Generalship of George E. Pickett After Gettysburg," in *Leadership and Command in the American Civil War*. CA: Campbell, 1996.

Gragg, Rod. *The Illustrated Confederate Reader*. New York: Gramercy Books, 1998.

Lanning, Michael Lee. *The Civil War 100*. Illinois: Sourcebooks, Inc., 2006.

Phillips, David. *Civil War Chronicles: Crucial Land Battles*. New York: MetroBooks, 1996.

Pickett Society website: http://www.pickettsociety.com/general.html accessed 10.01.2012.

Robbins, James S. *Last in Their Class: Custer, Pickett and the Goats of West Point*. New York: Encounter Books, 2006.

Sell, Bill. *Leaders of the North and South*. New York: MetroBooks, 1996.

Tagg, Larry. *The Generals of Gettysburg*. Campbell, CA: Savas Publishing, 1998.

Vectorsite.net, "July 1863 (3): Don't Forget Today That You Are From Old Virginia," http://www.vectorsite.net/twcw_51.html accessed 09.29.2012.

Waugh, John C. *The Class of 1846: From West Point to Appomattox: Stonewall Jackson, George McClellan, and Their Brothers*. New York: Warner Books, 1994.

Made in the USA
Middletown, DE
27 January 2018